Mission

'Technology is fundamentally changing the way people live, work and travel, and a new generation of innovative companies has emerged in recent years. In *Mission*, Michael Hayman and Nick Giles pinpoint the importance of social purpose to the entrepreneurs and businesses who are transforming societies around the world. It is mission that makes successful businesses stand out, and this book shows how companies are able to define, build and communicate their purpose in order to prosper'

Joe Gebbia, Co-founder and Chief Product Officer, Airbnb

'*Mission* shows how purpose has become essential to today's business leaders. Capitalism can best flourish if based on new, ethical and socially motivated foundations and this book shows why purpose-driven businesses are winning out, and acting as a force for good in society'

John Mackey, founder, Whole Foods

'*Mission* makes a compelling case for purpose as the defining ingredient of today's most successful businesses that are able to move from "ideation" to "global scale".
In the battle for talent, it is a central commercial purpose that sorts the great from the good. Any business that wants to stand out in today's crowded market needs to ask themselves what they are really trying to achieve and why their company matters. This book shows you how mission is a critical tool for leaders serious about scaling their business into a global player'

**Sherry Coutu, Non-executive Director,
London Stock Exchange**

'The grasp of the reality that every business should be a force for good in offering solutions to society's challenges is a fault line between our current different generations. This book will help its readers see with clarity what the future of successful business already looks like.

This book clearly sets out why those businesses built on profits and social purpose will win as they attract engaged customers, employees and investors, and are born from twenty-first century, values-led, entrepreneurs'

Paul Lindley, founder, Ella's Kitchen

'It is obvious to me that we need to support those who are going to create wealth for our nation and to do this we need to encourage new entrepreneurs and deliver the conditions in which, young people especially, can attain the skills, education and experiences that will stand them in good stead should they choose to become enterprising and entrepreneurial. Quite apart from the basics and supporting start-up companies, we need to really get behind those companies that show real promise and begin to grow fast. A concentration of effort in support of these companies, and especially the people who are behind them, is the best way that we can create the big global companies that are needed to create the wealth that the UK needs to be prosperous. In *Mission*, Michael Hayman and Nick Giles show very clearly why standout companies are increasingly defined by purpose and the ambition to effect positive change.

'It is very clear to me that a new generation of young companies is emerging that, with the correct conditions created in this country by everyone standing up to support them in their entrepreneurial endeavours, are going to be the job creators and wealth creators this country needs.

This book is an apt appreciation of the business culture that is developing and has developed in the UK over recent years, one in which I have seen its authors play an important role in cultivating'

HRH The Duke of York, KG

ABOUT THE AUTHORS

Michael Hayman and Nick Giles are the co-founders of Seven Hills, the highly acclaimed campaigns firm. The business was founded to generate momentum for Britain's fast-growing companies and most exciting entrepreneurs. The firm was named the Best Corporate Consultancy in the world by the Holmes Report and is also a Santander Breakthrough 50 winner.

Michael is a co-founder of StartUp Britain, the national initiative for early-stage enterprise launched by the Prime Minister. He is Chairman of Entrepreneurs at the private bank Coutts and an Honorary Fellow at the University of Cambridge Judge Business School. He was awarded an MBE for services to enterprise promotion in 2014.

Nick works closely with high growth firms in the UK, US and Asia. He is an ambassador for the Hong Kong government's venture programme. He is also an advisory board member of Tech London Advocates and is an advisor to the global youth movement One Young World.

Michael and Nick were listed in *GQ* magazine's inaugural 100 most connected men.

Mission

How the Best in Business Break Through

MICHAEL HAYMAN
AND NICK GILES

PORTFOLIO
PENGUIN

PORTFOLIO PENGUIN

UK | USA | Canada | Ireland | Australia
India | New Zealand | South Africa

Portfolio Penguin is part of the Penguin Random House group of companies
whose addresses can be found at global.penguinrandomhouse.com.

First published 2015

001

Copyright © Michael Hayman and Nick Giles, 2015

The moral right of the authors has been asserted

Set in 12.5/14.75 pt Garamond MT Std
Typeset by Jouve (UK), Milton Keynes
Printed in Great Britain by Clays Ltd, St Ives plc

A CIP catalogue record for this book is available from the British Library

HARDBACK ISBN: 978–0–241–00477–7
TRADE PAPERBACK ISBN: 978–0–241–24265–0

www.greenpenguin.co.uk

Contents

Introduction

In today's business world, mission matters.

It gives you the purpose to succeed in our unstable, fast-changing and challenging environment. A changing world where it has been said that two thirds of the companies that will make up the S&P 500 stock market index in a decade's time have yet to be created.

Consider the words of Winston Churchill, Britain's wartime leader. 'The empires of the future are the empires of the mind,' he said in 1943. Over seven decades on, that prophecy is being fulfilled in a commercial sense, because today's business world has become a battleground: for attention, preference and ideas. A battle for the mind in which companies must seek purpose as well as profit.

In this attention economy, breaking through is everything: the ability to connect with the consumer, the employee and the shareholder.

Central to mission is the rise of a new commercial currency: belief. It is a bond of trust with the consumer and marketplace that transcends the cynicism that so many have towards brand messages and advertising.

At its most potent, a driving mission defines and differentiates you. It brings to life an activist mentality and it marks out the most exciting and successful businesses of today. And with it comes the promise of a rare business gift – momentum. This is the force to build businesses, to move markets, to mobilize and motivate. To drive progress. Make no mistake, it is business leaders with a mission and a big idea who can really change the world. Take Airbnb, the rental marketplace changing how we think about our homes; Uber, transforming transportation; and Google, finding new ways to understand the world.

These are innovative, breakthrough companies, which share the vital asset of mission. Google, famously, was defined in its early years 'to organize the world's information and to make it universally accessible and useful'. Uber defines its mission to be 'transportation as reliable as running water, everywere and for everyone.' Airbnb simply states that it wants to allow its users to 'belong anywhere'.

Through mission, ideas are translated into a practical purpose that drives a company forward. It lends a clarity and directness to the everyday operations of a business, through what advertising legends the Saatchi brothers once described as the 'brutal simplicity of thought'.

Mission provides the basis for the belief that a business must inspire in those who work for, invest in or buy from it: the bonds of trust that are harder than ever to forge in a crowded and cynical marketplace. It is that shared and common belief which is at the heart of the businesses we will explore in this book.

What we have observed is that these companies have mission in their commercial DNA. But the intention alone is not enough. To break through, mission must be intertwined with the zeal of a new class of capitalist, the campaigner.

Campaigners are the innovators, motivators and disruptors of the business world, whose pursuit of profit is enhanced by a driving and fundamental mission. People with the singular ambition to make a difference, who are changing the way we live and work.

Business campaigners move beyond the realm of mere ambition, turning mission into a market reality that changes people's lives. There is something of the political campaigner in many of them. They have mastered the art of narrative and storytelling to turn their cause into something that brings supporters and advocates in its wake. The companies they create are underpinned by a culture that develops and sustains the original mission, binding employees and customers alike to the cause.

Campaigners weave narratives that imagine and move towards a better world. Their offer is a fundamentally optimistic counterpoint to the cynicism and crisis that fills news bulletins on a daily basis. They are creators, merchants and communicators of ideas.

They are at their roots optimists. Leaders whose inspiration from mission is matched by determined action; often gifted communicators who can turn an idea into a tangible reality; conveners who build a following, an enfranchised tribe of the hopeful to sustain and grow the vision. They are an emerging generation of commercial champions, and this book is dedicated to exploring their world.

Commercial campaigners break through, because the

value and growth potential of business is increasingly determined by future promise and the successful marriage of profit and purpose.

One study estimated that 80 per cent of the value of S&P 500 companies in 2010 was made up of intangible assets: intellectual property, identity, reputation and brand, where products and services once ruled. It is an environment where the ability to explain your proposition is paramount, your narrative matters and the best story wins.

Campaigners get this. Great companies must inspire confidence but there is an equal need to evoke strong feelings. Feeling is an asset that is easily dismissed by the cynical. Yet it is the key to belief and it is belief that leads to action, which is at the heart of change. And from supermarkets to stock markets, feeling is what mints the increasingly vital currency of belief.

That matters more than ever, because we live in an unprecedentedly uncertain world, bombarded by information from all around us. In the words of Juan Enriquez, the former CEO of Mexico City's Urban Development Corporation: 'Today a street stall in Mumbai can access more information, maps, statistics, academic papers, price trends, future markets and data than a US president could only a few decades ago.'

It is an arena that is made for the mission-driven campaigner, those with simplicity and purity of purpose, clarity of vision and an unquenchable determination to deliver.

Product alone will not get you noticed in this age of

attention drought. If you want to stand out you need to stand for something. To thirst for change. To campaign for attention and support.

The argument of *Mission* is that the environment for business has changed and that the traits of successful companies have had to evolve in turn. The world is moving at a faster pace than ever before; consumers are information rich but time poor; the marketplace is harsher and more demanding. It's a world where the hazy complexities of modernity lead to a fog of uncertainty. Where today's success story can be trashed in moments; where the scrutiny of a 24-hour media has been enhanced by the rapid rise of Twitter.

Faced by these conditions, companies must campaign to get noticed and stay ahead: to achieve profit through distilling and manifesting purpose.

We have observed three underlying traits shared by businesses that are thriving in this new world:

A driving desire to change things, a higher purpose that drives profit.

Turning the mission into a powerful reality. The activist mentality.

The measure of success, moving and growing faster than the competition.

More than ever before, great companies must be mission-based, and to make an impact in an impatient and cynical marketplace they must embrace the determined, optimistic outlook of the campaigner. You can measure their success through their momentum: speed of progress and growth relative to the market.

Through the purity of their mission, the strength of their ideas and the power of their storytelling, campaigners win the battle for attention, competing in markets of the mind.

Campaigning is a movement that is changing the fundamentals of how business operates, disrupting convention, creating explosive growth and new sources of capital. From the business campaigners we have met, worked alongside and interviewed for this book, we have identified three new commercial markets that are redefining business and bringing huge success to their creators:

Carers: Companies that want to change people's lives for the better, embracing consumers and the honest dialogue that many others fear;

Sharers: Companies that bring people together, taking advantage of the unparalleled networks that the Internet has created, changing the way we consume goods and services;

Darers: Companies that refuse to take no for an answer and who thrive on tackling the impossible at every turn, harnessing the growing power of technology to achieve the unthinkable.

We founded our business, Seven Hills, in the teeth of the recession at the beginning of 2010. And as the effects of the most damaging downturn since the 1930s begin to recede, the lesson we draw is this: the best in business are often defined by their sense of mission, a purpose that underpins the ability to make profit. It is because of this that they break through.

In the last five years we have observed and worked alongside entrepreneurs and growth companies on both sides of the Atlantic, in sectors ranging from big data to baby food. What we have learned we have also sought to practise: a campaigning approach in everything we do.

It has been, and continues to be, an extraordinary journey. It has provided us with a crow's nest view of the nation's high-growth firms and their quest for success. And it has helped us with a singular mission. To be the defining campaigning company.

What we have also learned in that time is that the campaigning mentality is one that goes well beyond how a business presents itself. It is born out of a defining sense of mission and belief, delivered with the intensity of the activist, and it provides the precious gift of market momentum.

We have worked with campaigners at the top of their game. In our first year, we were able to author a report led by Virgin's Sir Richard Branson and work with founding *Dragons' Den* panellist Peter Jones. Since then, we have worked alongside inspiring founders who include Paul Lindley of Ella's Kitchen; David Richards of WANdisco; Phil Libin of Evernote; and Cobra Beer's Lord Bilimoria.

We co-founded StartUp Britain, a national campaign

launched by the Prime Minister and fully supported by the Government, which has been at the heart of record levels of UK business creation; and have pioneered many of the most successful enterprise campaigns in Britain in the last five years.

These experiences have given us insight into what makes this thriving generation of campaigning individuals and businesses tick, what makes them different, and why they are prospering in a commercial environment that has laid low so many traditional businesses and institutions.

In *Mission*, we will tell the stories both of the companies we have worked with in the past five years and other business leaders who we interviewed for this book. They include Lord Rose, the former chief executive of Marks & Spencer; Joe Gebbia, founder of Airbnb; John Mackey, founder of Whole Foods; Sarah Wood, co-founder of Unruly; Dido Harding, CEO of TalkTalk; and Sir Terry Leahy, former CEO of Tesco.

What commercial campaigners stand for, how they do business, and what they hope to achieve has big implications for us all. This book is dedicated to identifying, exploring and sharing their arts.

Mission is for anyone with the entrepreneurial spirit, and for those who want to know how to unleash it. The embodiments of campaigning in business may be the founders and leaders of highly successful companies, but the lessons from that success can be learned and implemented in many different arenas, from aspirant entrepreneurs to corporate executives. This book seeks to inspire those who want to inject fresh energy and purpose into their working lives.

Based on the insights of those who have been there and done it, it is a guide for launching and growing a business or making a difference in your corporate job: realizing the potential for your business and career to break through, through mission, the campaigning way.

Mission is about being the best. Like any opportunity, the only real question is, are you going to take it?

I

Mission

*The reasonable man adapts himself to the world: the
unreasonable one persists in trying to adapt the world to himself.
Therefore all progress depends on the unreasonable man.*

George Bernard Shaw

We are witnessing the rise of the activist business. Airbnb co-founder Brian Chesky put it to the *Sunday Times* that he has 'a mission to create a world where anyone can belong anywhere. I've decided that's my life's work.' Many of today's breakthrough businesses are those with a clear purpose that sits alongside profit: how that is formulated and articulated to the market has become a vital element of commercial success. In the words of Amazon founder Jeff Bezos, whose story we will examine in this chapter, 'missionaries make better products.'

Of course, bold and fundamental missions have always had an important place in business. Outside Microsoft's Washington headquarters sits a stone plaque which reads, 'Every time a product ships, it takes us one step closer to the vision: a computer on every desk and in every home.'

This mission statement says much more about Microsoft's success than any program, operating system or user interface ever could. What it tells you is that Bill Gates and his founding team didn't just start out trying to make great software. They set out with a bold and daring vision of how they could make the world a better place. They set out with a mission, as campaigners.

As the Microsoft story shows, the importance of mission in business is not new. But its significance has been radically enhanced by changes in the environment for doing business that have altered the way companies and consumers interact. Customers now expect to be in direct dialogue with the brands they buy from. The power that comes through their online support can take a company from a fledgling start-up to a rising star in what seems no time at all. At the same time it creates a channel of communication that is out of the company's control and one complaint can easily become a trickle that grows into a flood.

The new reality for business is one where customers have significant influence to wield and their voices must be heard. In that context, a mission that customers treat as credible and worthy of their interest becomes disproportionately important.

Burning the Boats

The way companies communicate their mission is becoming an essential part of how they establish an authentic relationship with customers. Yet your mission must run much deeper than the external presentation: in the best companies it is hard-wired into the psyche and everyday running of the business.

Mission creates a binding sense of purpose in a venture that allows it to navigate the choppy waters of founding and growing a business. For new companies, it is the essential starting point, one that reflects the need for absolute certainty when launching a business.

At this stage, there can be no looking back, no half-measures, no dipping your toe in the water. You have to plunge right in. So it is no coincidence that those who succeed are the entrepreneurs with a crystalline mission: who know exactly where they want to go and how far their abilities can take them.

The importance of mission is well demonstrated by the story of the Spanish Conquistador Hernán Cortés. In 1519 he sailed his fleet to the coast of modern-day Mexico, to begin what would end in the conquest of the mighty Aztec empire. His initial force was a mere 620 men and his command on landing was this: 'Burn the boats.'

A brutal but vital order with a simple message: there can be no turning back, no looking over your shoulder or harking back to safety. One option. Forward to victory. It was a command that hardened souls and saved lives. The same is true in business today. Starting a company is a high-stakes risk and will often be the biggest gamble of an entrepreneur's life.

As David Richards, founder of big data company WANdisco, put it to *Elite Business* magazine in a 2013 interview:

'I refuse to give advice to people who say, "I'm going to wait and see if this works and then I'll give up my job." I won't even talk to them. The people who are really prepared to make that commitment, to take a risk that might impair them economically; that's my true definition of an entrepreneur.'

A mission is not something that every interested party will believe in or buy into. Many may seek to diminish or demean it. But it is hard to name businesses that succeed without that purpose being hard-wired at some level. The mission is what binds together the disparate players who make up a business and points them towards the matter at hand. Purpose is essential to creating and sustaining a company because none of your main actors – founders, employees, consumers – can really survive or thrive without it.

'Entrepreneurs . . . have to be missionaries for their ideas,' lastminute.com founder Martha Lane Fox told us. 'Some business leaders shy away from activism, but it's a mistake not to feel social as well as commercial purpose,' she believes.

Yet mission is something that cannot remain locked in the head of a founder or chief executive. At its most apparent, it is embodied by all those who work at a company, as a set of common values and beliefs that govern the everyday running of the firm.

Most people have had at least one job where the unrelenting tedium of the day-to-day grind becomes an almost overwhelming burden. Against this, a company with clear mission can be liberating and empowering; a place where the ambition to be brilliant and meaningful is fundamental and your place in that is valued.

The Speed Spiral

To understand why mission has become increasingly important to the new and growing companies of today, it is essential to realize how significantly the landscape for business has changed and the response that is demanded from companies.

If you want to understand what it means to be in business today, consider this: the most powerful companies of your lifetime are likely to be ones you may not yet have heard of. In many cases, they are probably yet to be created.

For a taste of how that might look, go back ten years: YouTube had just been founded, Facebook was little over a year old, Twitter still yet to be launched. These are businesses that within a decade of starting up have become commercial icons of their day, not to mention everyday tools of conversation and interaction.

Today, the effect is even more marked. The *Wall Street Journal*'s list of 'billion-dollar start-ups' shows companies rising to stratospheric valuations within a few years of having been launched. Photo messaging app Snapchat, founded in 2012, was a $10 billion company two years later. While previously business winners might have taken a generation to build, today they are being scaled with equivalent commercial impact and world-leading potential in just a few years.

In business, you can no longer be too young to understand or too small to make a difference. It is an era where teenagers can become business titans. Take Nick D'Aloisio, a seventeen-year-old who created and sold a business for more millions (19) than he had years, when Yahoo acquired his news aggregation app Summly in 2013. The economy has levelled out and created opportunities for new entrants that never previously existed. When the FTSE 100 index celebrated its thirtieth anniversary in 2014, for instance, just thirty of the original membership had survived.

But the world hasn't just speeded up in the past few decades; it has also become rich with information to the point of saturation. The Nobel Prize-winning economist Herbert Simon wrote as far back as 1977 that 'a wealth of information creates a poverty of attention.' Almost four decades later that has become truer than even Simon probably imagined possible. According to the authors of *The Human Face of Big Data*, 'The average person today processes more data in a single day than a person in the 1500s did in an entire lifetime.' And the US National Center for Biotechnology Information suggests the average human attention span declined by four seconds between 2000 and 2013, down from twelve seconds to eight. That means we can concentrate less well than the average goldfish, which can manage nine seconds.

We are truly attention-poor, bloated by information

and starved of the capacity to process or understand it all. This makes the battle for attention the very front line of your business. A business without an audacious mission that will make consumers sit up and take notice will increasingly struggle to make its mark. It is the only way of cutting through the maelstrom of competing noise to get a case heard.

What follows are the stories of three very different companies and how they have been defined by mission. Online retail platform Amazon, ethical clothing brand Patagonia and restaurant chain Leon may on the surface have little in common. Patagonia is a widely admired company while Amazon, despite its undoubted status as an innovator and market leader, has attracted controversy on everything from how it treats its workers to copyright infringement, competition laws and the products it sells. Leon is little more than a decade old while Patagonia was founded in 1973, and Amazon in 1994.

Yet what unites the three is the success they have had, in large part due to the driving mission that was embedded within all three companies by their founders from the very beginning. Like them or not, these are companies that have sought to bring about a radical change in how people and indeed companies think and act: be that to harness the limitless potential of the Internet or to use commercial success to repair some of the environmental damage humans and corporations have caused. They show what mission in action can achieve.

The Missionary Entrepreneur: Jeff Bezos and Amazon

In the original Amazon.com office, the computers were programmed to ring a bell whenever a book was sold. It was a nice touch in the founding period of the business, when daily sales were in single figures, but by late 2012, the orders were flying in at a rate of 306 per second, or 26.5 million in all on the record-beating day of 27 November 2014. It is no surprise that the bell has not survived.

Amazon's hard-fought success can be summed up by a URL that founder Jeff Bezos registered in 1995: Relentless.com (try it, you will end up in a familiar place). What it symbolizes is the burning ambition of a company for whom online bookselling was merely a means to an end: the entire e-commerce market, or the 244 million people who bought items through Amazon in the last year.

As an early employee told *The New York Times* in 2013, 'For many of us, creating Earth's biggest bookstore would have been enough. Jeff's goal was a touch grander: "to conquer the world".' Bezos himself speaks about his company in the evangelical language of the true-believing campaigner: 'I strongly believe that missionaries make better products,' he told *Fortune* magazine in 2010. 'They care more. For a missionary, it's not just about the business . . . you do it because you have something meaningful that motivates you.'

What appears to motivate the Amazon founder above all is discovery. In a letter to early shareholders after the company's IPO in 1997, Bezos pondered the potential of the industry that his company had started to create: 'This is Day 1 for the Internet and, if we execute well, for Amazon.com,' he wrote. 'Today, online commerce saves customers money and precious time. Tomorrow, through personalization, online commerce will accelerate the very process of discovery.'

Four paragraphs into the letter, six italicized words spelled out the philosophy that has defined the company ever since: *'It's all about the long-term.'* It is why a company that sees sales of nigh on $20 billion per quarter routinely turns little or no profit, reinvesting revenue into fields that have ranged from e-readers to cloud computing, robotics, TV production and grocery delivery.

Amazon symbolizes that new breed of company we touched upon in the Introduction – one that exists not just to make money but to create products, shape services and develop ideas that are life changing for consumers. The Amazon mission is as simple and wide-ranging as the Internet itself: to mine the full potential of what history's greatest ever network can achieve.

As Brad Stone, author of a book on the company, wrote in 2013: '[Bezos] believes the opportunity offered by the Internet, and by e-commerce, is massive and still largely untapped. To him, it's still a land grab.'

Two decades after he left a safe Wall Street perch to create Amazon, Bezos has become one of the defining entrepreneurs of the Internet era: the early adopter who has set an unrelenting pace ever since; the disruptor who built a behemoth, without losing his urge to innovate, build and discover.

As Bezos has often admitted, not every new idea is a good one and relatively few will yield commercial success. But the overriding lesson is not to let the prospect or reality of failure get in the way of your mission. 'You have to be super clear about what kind of company you're trying to build,' he told a *Business Insider* conference in 2014. 'We said we were going to take big bets. We said we were going to fail.' What the Amazon story shows is that staying true to your mission is the best protection against the slings and arrows that assail every business. Don't let failure put you off pursuing the full limits of your big idea.

Environmental Activists: Yvon Chouinard and Patagonia

If doing better by customers is the motivation behind many brands, then doing better by the planet is another notable source of purpose. In 1973, Yvon Chouinard founded outdoor clothing brand Patagonia, starting out in the blacksmith's shop he owned in Ventura, California. It is a company with social mission at its core.

'Together we reimagine a world where we take only what nature can replace,' reads its website, highlighting that human activity expends natural resources around 1.5 times as fast as nature can replace them.

Its mission is to 'make the best product with the least environmental impact and the most social value possible'. Accordingly, the brand focuses on using high-quality materials that ensure a long life and usability for their garments and promises to replace, repair or help resell all of its products. Indeed Patagonia's website describes the team as 'environmental activists' and it now advises giants including Walmart on reducing the impact of packaging and water waste.

Chouinard, who has been hailed as 'America's most unlikely business guru', has become a flag bearer for the idea that business can be a vehicle for social and environmental good. 'I never even wanted to be in business,' he told the *Wall Street Journal* in 2012. 'But I hang onto Patagonia because it's my resource to do something good. It's a way to demonstrate that corporations can lead examined lives.'

The brand's commitment to combating waste and publicizing the environmental impact of business extends to an ad campaign, headlined 'Don't buy this jacket'. Recounting the water, carbon dioxide and waste costs of making just one of its bestselling R2 jackets, the ad concluded: 'As is true of all the things we make and you can buy, this jacket comes with an environmental cost higher than its price . . . Don't buy what you don't need.'

Patagonia also prides itself on a range of campaigns to achieve and promote environmental sustainability, including the Common Threads Partnership to reduce the collective environmental footprint through repair, reuse and recycling of materials.

Since 1985 the company has donated an annual 1 per cent of its sales to environmental organizations, a self-styled 'earth tax', over $41 million in all. Through the social action group, '1% for the Planet', it has also brought together over 1,200 companies that share the same pledge.

Chouinard stands out as an entrepreneur who demands a high standard not only of himself but of his customers and competitors. In 1991 he was advised to sell the company after its rapid growth was stopped in its tracks, and 120 employees had to be let go. As he said to the *Wall Street Journal*: 'I decided the best thing I could do was to get profitable again, live a more examined corporate life and influence other companies to do the same.'

As a principled and purposeful company with a mission to change the environmental behaviour of individuals and corporations across the world, Patagonia epitomizes the kind of business that is thriving in today's turbulent global economy. Its story shows the willingness of consumers to support a business based around a set of authentic beliefs, and that trust can be as important as price and promotion in the retail market.

'If God Did Fast Food': the Leon Mission

Not every business mission need be about changing the world or righting great global wrongs. Indeed many of the best companies you will encounter emerged from a very personal frustration about gaps in the market, which motivated entrepreneurs then sought to fill. Nor does it need to be set in stone right from the start. 'Naturally' fast-food chain Leon is a successful company that emerged not from a grandiose vision for change, but from a very simple, everyday need, which has become a stylish business whose activist scope has grown in step with it.

For John Vincent and Henry Dimbleby, colleagues at the management consultancy Bain & Company, that frustration was the lack of appealing and healthy eating options on their frequent away trips.

'We started Leon because we were travelling a lot,' Henry told the business website *Smarta*. 'We wanted to eat fast food on the go and all we could eat was either really cold sandwiches, in slightly grim neon-lit chiller cabinets, or really delicious, greasy fast food that tasted great then made you fall asleep.

'We thought, why can't there be good fast food: fast food that tastes good and does you good?'

As his business partner put it in the same interview: 'you have to have a simple idea that drives you and that touchstone for us was "If God did fast food". If God did fast food, it would be a bit like fast food, but in some ways it would be completely different. We had this image that you maybe die, go to heaven, you have art class with Leonardo da Vinci, and then he says let's go to a fast food joint. And the idea was, OK, what would it be like?

'It would be uncannily like a fast food joint in its processes, the fact that it would use a kitchen and a chute, but it would be fantastic ingredients going through that system, just as tasty, served by people in a warm environment [who] didn't have a script, but speak from the heart. And that was what drove us.'

That was the starting point for giving up their well-paid

jobs to launch a venture, in 2004, which has now swelled to a twenty-two-restaurant chain, sweeping up a breadth of awards along the way, with reviews describing it as 'a miracle' and 'a place where you can have your cake and eat it.'

Yet the very simple mission that converted two management consultants into one of the UK's most innovative restaurant duos has both remained the driving force behind Leon and expanded as the company has grown.

The campaigning passion of the pair has taken them beyond business. In 2012, Vincent and Dimbleby were recruited to advise the government on improving the standards and nutrition of UK school dinners.

Their concluding report focused on the 'damage that is being done to the nation's health, happiness and finances by bad diet' and highlighted 'the benefits of introducing children to a good food culture as early as possible.'

In other words, the founding mission of Leon had become the basis of a clarion call for the health of the nation and in particular children. What began as a shared frustration at the inability to get a square meal on the road, has become a campaigning company which seeks not just to provide good lunches, but to change the way the country thinks about food and nutrition.

What's Your Mission?

So how can you best identify, communicate and harness the mission at the heart of your company? You need to start by trying to answer the difficult but simple question that was once posed to us: 'What does your business stand for?' More than ever, the longer it takes you to answer that question, or the more evasive you are about it, the less well equipped you are for success.

The second thing is to write it down. Tony Blair's former communications chief Alastair Campbell now advises large organizations on getting their message right, and has written about his method for working with clients. He asks the senior team to fill out postcards that read 'the main objective of our organization is . . .' on one side, and 'the strategy to meet our objective is . . .' on the reverse. 'Nine times out of ten, I gather in a stack of different objectives, strategies which are tactics, or strategies which are objectives', he says.

This is a brilliant exercise that demonstrates the essential link between purpose and outcome. If the people around the boardroom table don't buy into your founding belief, or worse, don't understand it, then what chance does the business have?

The postcard exercise is one that companies large and small should make full use of. Beyond a small team of founders working in the same room, it is unlikely that in a company of any size there will be absolute accord over what it is your business is fundamentally trying to achieve: the communication of your mission, external and internal, requires careful and constant curation.

Try the postcard question and compare the responses you get. You would be surprised that even among people who work very closely together, there may be very different ideas about the mission and direction of the company. That could be for a whole variety of reasons: true, in certain cases an important anchorage may have been lost along the way, but it is equally possible that circumstances have changed sufficiently to demand a change in direction and a new course.

Easily discernible from the outside, this can often come as a major shock to those at the heart of the business. Advising a multi-national, one of us once settled on the ploy of gathering together the various different business cards from across the group. Not one of them bore any resemblance to any of the others, and the CEO was appalled.

In extreme cases, the question may not even be 'what do you stand for?', but quite simply, 'what are you doing?' That was the poser faced by Dame Marjorie Scardino when she assumed control of Pearson in 1997.

'When I got here there were theme parks, and Madame Tussauds and we even found an avocado farm,' she told the *Sunday Times* after her retirement in 2012. 'Those were things you'd have to stretch very hard to fit into a strategy.'

Her response was clear, as the 1997 annual report for the company demonstrates. 'Simpler things cut cleanly through resistance, moving faster and more efficiently toward their destination,' she wrote under the headline, 'It's hard to simplify complicated things'. Yet that was exactly what she managed, disposing of extraneous, conflicting assets to focus on the education business, which was three quarters of the entire company by the time she stepped away.

Fast forward from Scardino's first annual report to her last, in 2011, and the fruits of that simplification are evident. 'For more than a decade now, Pearson's strategy has revolved around our commitment to become the leading global learning company,' it reads. 'The company saw tremendous social and economic need for education and skills, giving rise to significant business opportunities. We have therefore initiated – and continue to pursue – a radical shift in our business portfolio towards education.'

What Dame Marjorie achieved in her sixteen-year tenure was a remarkable feat of business alchemy. She turned a sprawling group into a business that truly owns its definition as the world's foremost education company. She gave Pearson a mission, around the dissemination of knowledge and ideas, that has acted as its guiding star ever since.

By the time she vacated the chief executive's chair, turnover and profits had trebled. As important, Pearson had earned a market position with real equity. It transformed into a brand with purpose, because a strong leader made sure they got the story right.

The 'About Us' section of its website now carries a quote from Albert Einstein: 'If you can't explain it simply enough, you don't understand it well enough.' Scardino helped Pearson understand better what it should be about. She restored its mission.

Every good business story begins with mission. It is

something that demands regular and consistent attention: a code of belief and values to be maintained, developed and shared. As the examples above have shown, the mission you start out with can be fundamentally the same even decades later. But just as no successful business is a stagnant one, mission cannot be a static entity. It grows, reshapes and evolves along with the company and organization it supports. Taking frequent opportunities to discuss, develop and write down the mission that underpins annual and ongoing targets is the surest way of avoiding the fate of companies that lose their way or never really find it in the first place.

Once you have captured and defined your mission, you need to put it into action and embrace the activist mentality of the commercial campaigner. Next we will look at how a generation of entrepreneurs changed the way business is done, how the campaigning approach they pioneered is being developed today and what it can do for your business.

Takeaways

- Today's thriving entrepreneurs are those motivated by a mission to change things for the better, through their businesses;
- Often these missions are about achieving the seemingly impossible. In fact, it is their very audacity that gives the business its missionary zeal;

- Starting a business is a high-stake risk but such is an entrepreneur's sense of purpose that they will be 100 per cent committed, right from the start. They will burn their boats;
- A business will all too often flounder without a central mission to galvanize its people and give it a common purpose. Be sure everyone knows what your founding mission is and how that purpose has evolved over time.

2

Campaigning

Go big or go home. Because it's true.
What do you have to lose?

Eliza Dushku

A mission that inspires belief is a fundamental ingredient
for today's businesses. But to grow, that mission must be
communicated in a way that convinces the most important audiences – your customers and employees – that this
is a company worth investing either their money or their
life in. If the first fundamental part of being successful in
business today is having a clear mission, then the second
is becoming a commercial campaigner.

Campaigning is the mode by which your business mission is put into action and made real. It is a term most
obviously associated with politics, and in this chapter we
will explore the emergence of the activist entrepreneur as
a phenomenon that grew out of a deeply political era in
the 1970s and 1980s.

The lessons for business from politics remain as pertinent today. Running your office has, in many ways,

become akin to running for public office, convincing customers much as candidates seek to persuade voters. The challenges for business today – to inspire belief in a cynical marketplace, manage the pace of change and respond to the increasing demands of customers – are those that have always been the preserve of politicians. Indeed, the campaigning imperative is one that now unites the worlds of business and government: Daniel Korski, special adviser to Prime Minister David Cameron, put it to us that, 'the only way in which we in government can change things, take ideas from inception to delivery, is ourselves to become campaigners.'

In today's ultra-competitive marketplace, where companies must battle for attention before they can start to contest sales, it is a powerful option to approach your business like an election candidate. Just as politicians have historically been society's consummate campaigners, now it is entrepreneurs and business leaders who have learned to shape a message that connects and persuades, an affirmative narrative that outlines the possibility of a better world, and a belief that the conveyor of the promise can deliver upon it.

In subsequent chapters we will take a detailed look at the characteristics of the campaigner and how you can awaken this mentality within your business. But we begin with the generation of 1970s and 1980s entrepreneurs who we consider to have established campaigning as a new approach to business: Steve Jobs of Apple, Richard Branson of Virgin and John Mackey of Whole Foods. Three companies that continue to prosper today, their early days merit close examination for the lessons to be learned about steeping a business in mission, campaigning for ideas that were initially dismissed as unfashionable, and ultimately overcoming both their competitors and their detractors.

All three were the products of their time, emerging out of a decade of social upheaval with a driving mission to make the world a better place through the companies they built. Apple, founded in 1976, Virgin, founded in 1970, and Whole Foods, founded in 1980, were all created by entrepreneurs who had in many ways been shaped by the events of the 1960s.

In *The Apple Revolution*, author Luke Dormehl traces the rise of Apple out of the Vietnam War and Woodstock era counterculture: 'The rise of the personal computer from its humble, garage-born roots to the vast industry that it currently represents is, in a very real sense, the forgotten part of the counterculture story,' he wrote. 'It is all too easy to pass over the contributions of the wireheads, phreakers, cyberpunks and other techno-geeks who seized upon the countercultural revolution as their opportunity to claim high-tech for the masses.'

Reflecting on his first business venture, Sir Richard Branson, Virgin's founder, later wrote that: 'I started *Student* magazine as a teenager. Nothing to do with being a businessman, I just wanted to run a magazine, have fun doing it and try to help the campaign to stop the Vietnamese war. I wanted to do something that I thought would be entertaining and fun.'

Meanwhile, John Mackey, founder of Whole Foods, recalled in a 2004 speech that 'my search for meaning and purpose led me into the counterculture movement of the late 1960s and 1970s . . . I'm one of those crunchy granola types.' Now the owner of an international company employing over 58,000 people with stores in almost 400 locations, Mackey was originally dismissed as 'just selling hippy food to hippies'.

Apple, Virgin and Whole Foods epitomize the first generation of campaigning companies. They were products of a rebellious age, started by entrepreneurs who sought to make the world a better place through the missions their companies had been built on. 'A business is an idea of somebody's to make people's lives better,' Branson told an *Inc* magazine conference in 2013. 'The only reason we've succeeded is because we've made other people's lives better.' John Mackey expressed a very similar sentiment when interviewed by Michael at a packed town hall debate in Austin, Texas: 'Entrepreneurs are fundamentally very creative individuals,' he said. 'They have a sense of higher purpose. They're not in it primarily to make money, that's a secondary concern. They're in it to fulfil their dreams and their passions.'

These are companies with big ideas at their core. For Apple, it is the democratization of the power of computing; for Virgin, the big idea is to be a challenger business to corporate behemoths; while for Whole Foods it is about a healthier society.

What these business icons of the baby boomer

generation represented was a broadening of the entrepreneurial opportunity and the realization that the power to change things sat not with the traditional organs of corporate or state power, but with those motivated to create something from nothing.

'You have to remember that in the 1970s, profit was seen as theft,' recalls Lord Young, serial entrepreneur and enterprise adviser to the UK Prime Minister in the 2010–15 Parliament. Now entrepreneurs are lauded, from corporate boardrooms to Downing Street and the White House, for their valuable contribution to the economic and social life of a country.

This generation of entrepreneurs pioneered an insurgent mentality within the commercial sphere that is a direct forebear of the campaigning style of so many successful companies today. Their belief was that business could be better and do better at the same time. Their early-years stories remain an important reference point for anyone wanting to know why campaigning makes a difference in business and how a company can succeed by building a mission into a powerful campaign that inspires belief, builds a following and ultimately effects change.

The Pioneers: Think Different

'Taking LSD was a profound experience, one of the most important things in my life. LSD shows you that there's another side to the coin . . . It reinforced my sense of what was important – creating great things instead of making money, putting things back into the stream of history and of human consciousness as much as I could.' These are not the words you might expect of one of the twenty-first century's foremost business leaders. And whatever you might think of Apple co-founder Steve Jobs' reminiscence, it reveals an essential context to the origins of Apple as one of the pioneering campaigning companies.

A child of the 1960s, a disciple of Bob Dylan, Jobs' approach to business was irrevocably shaped by the music and culture he was raised with. 'The people who invented the twenty-first century were pot-smoking, sandal-wearing hippies from the West Coast like Steve,' Jobs' biographer Walter Isaacson has said. 'The sixties produced an anarchic mind-set that [was] great for imagining a world not yet in existence.'

Jobs was among a small group of entrepreneurs who envisaged the full potential of the personal computing market as the technology began to become available in the early 1970s. An innovator and market leader, he was also a campaigner with a driving mission, which was to level the odds between the corporation and the consumer. His quest – to be achieved through Apple – was to put as much computing power in the hands of every individual as had been at the unique command of privileged institutions.

This was a mission informed by a very clear sense of empowering the individual. It was a theme he returned to in his graduation address to Stanford University students in 2005: 'Your time is limited, so don't waste it living someone else's life. Don't be trapped by dogma – which is living with the results of other people's thinking. Don't let the noise of others' opinions drown out your own inner voice. And most important, have the courage to follow your heart and intuition. They somehow already know what you truly want to become.'

The 1990s 'Think Different' campaign may be the Apple advertising that most of us remember, but the advert that best captured the disruptive, rebellious, individualistic urge of the company in its early days was the Macintosh promotion that aired during half-time of the 1984 Super Bowl. Directed by Ridley Scott, it quite literally took aim at IBM. Into a lecture theatre filled with faceless, bald men being hectored by a Big Brother figure, emerges a female runner who hurls a sledgehammer at the controlling presence, who then explodes into a flash of light. Jobs wanted to share his vision of tearing down the pedestal of a corporation he saw as stifling, stale and a straitjacket on progress and used the biggest annual audience in American television to do so.

For Apple, the unifying attraction has, from the beginning, been one of adventure and discovery, and it remains its greatest selling point. The iPod may not have been the first or the best MP3 player, but that was how most customers perceived it to be, putting their money behind something that went beyond product and industrial design – the tribal urge to be at the head of a trend, to be part of a campaign.

That is very much tied into the voyaging spirit of a

company that was founded in opposition to a corporation that has often won heads, but never hearts, perhaps best summed up by the timeless aphorism that 'nobody ever got fired for buying IBM.'

The early Apple story is a quintessential case study of campaigning in action: for the idea of personal computing, in the hands of the mass market, against the grain of the corporate giants and against the tide of informed opinion that held this was a hobbyists' market that would never catch on. It drew on a fundamental mission – to democratize the power of computing – and the ethos and promotion of the company was as a challenger to the institutions which held that power.

The Pioneers: Screw It, Let's Do It

One word has always been sufficient to sum up the Virgin group, one of the UK's most identifiable campaigning companies: adventure.

It is a quality that has, throughout the lifetime of the company, been embodied by its flamboyant founder. Sir Richard Branson's catchphrase, 'Screw It, Let's Do It', has been the driving belief underpinning every twist and turn of a group that has amassed some 400 companies. Many undoubtedly succeed but a great many fail, and that is an integral part of the Virgin way.

Branson's core purpose is based on his commitment to people and personal freedoms. Take a look at one of his businesses, airlines, and you get a sense of how even an industry that has a fragile relationship with both of these, can show purpose in action. As he has written: 'When we went into the airline business, we went into it because we hated flying other people's airlines and we wanted to try something different. We thought we could create the kind of airline that I would like to fly, where people who flew on it could enjoy the experience and where the people who work for the airline would be proud of it.'

The launch of Virgin America took the market by storm, and at the heart of its success was its ability to bring innovation into the realm of the mundane. Air travel is dead time; it's the cramped interlude of rubbish food and monotonous safety demonstrations between two places you want to be. But this is not how Branson saw things.

In the summer of 2010, he landed in Dallas, Texas, kitted out in full cowboy regalia. As the state's bigwigs feasted on barbecued ribs beside a paddock of long-horned cattle to the sound of a set from country star Willie Nelson, Branson had a simple story to tell: 'Virgin America is here. Don't fly like cattle.' This bold PR stunt struck at the heart of what people care about in their everyday lives, presenting a challenge to the dull, soulless domestic airline experience, and brought innovation to a place no one thought it could exist.

As Branson explains: 'American carriers are all very much the same, and the people who run them do not think of the customers at all ... It's become a bus service ... If everything is a joy, if you come onto a plane and the lighting is right, the seating is right, and the cabin crew is happy, you feel welcome ... It's like you have come into somebody's home.'

Branson has found a corner of people's lives that they thought had to be boring and unpleasant and offered an alternative; a challenge to the status quo. Take, for example, the obligatory in-flight safety video. You'd be hard pressed to imagine how tips on wearing your seatbelt correctly could ever be exciting. But as soon as Virgin America's all-singing, all-dancing (literally) video begins with the lines:

> I've got some safety tips that you gotta know
> And trust me it's something that you wanna hear
> So honey, zip your lips and enjoy the show
> Before we move into the stratosphere,

you can hardly understand how predecessors got it so wrong. American Airlines' safety video has 118,000 views on YouTube; Virgin America's has over 10.5 million. One customer blogged about his experience in the following way: 'It never gets old boarding a Virgin America flight. Where most other airlines welcome you with white lighting (snoozers), Virgin America gives you a pink and purple feast for the eyes.'

That, in a nutshell, is what Branson and Virgin are all about. As he has written, 'This desire to do something different, take risks and challenge convention has been at the heart of the Virgin story from the very beginning.'

Battling airlines might be different to opening a record store on Oxford Street, but the underlying philosophy remains very much the same. A campaigning, activist will to achieve the impossible, invert the status quo and become distinctive in a sea of sameness.

The Pioneers: Conscious Capitalism

Many successful entrepreneurs are accused of taking their work home with them. John Mackey was one business-man who took his home with him to work. It was 1978 in Austin, Texas, and John Mackey had taken the plunge of opening his own grocery store. Mackey's passion was for food: after university, he had ended up living in a collect-ive and becoming the de facto cook: 'I loved being around food,' he told the *New Yorker* in 2010. 'I loved natural foods. I loved organic foods. And a thought entered my mind that this is what I could do.'

Mackey, who also worked part-time at a natural food store in the town, decided to take the plunge. Together with his then girlfriend, he scrimped together $45,000 to open Safer Way, a pun on the then leading supermarket Safeway. Such was the initial cashflow situation that Mackey moved in above the shop and came up with an ingenious solution for its lack of bathroom facilities: he'd use the hose from the dishwasher to shower himself down.

Two years later, Mackey merged with another local food store: the result was Whole Foods Market, a

10,000-square-foot store in a former nightclub. The emphasis was on natural and organic food, but the shop was different to other natural food stores. Today, with multiple acquisitions under its belt, Whole Foods has over 400 branches in the US, Canada and the UK.

In one sense the underlying Whole Foods campaign could be characterized around the importance of healthy food, natural ingredients and sustainable food production. Whole Foods describes itself as a 'company that aims to set the standards of excellence for food retailers'. And while its overall imprint in the food market remains minuscule, its impact has been out of proportion with its scale, contributing to increased demand for organic food, and greater awareness of sustainability and the effects of additives and chemicals.

Yet as John Mackey made clear in his book, *Conscious Capitalism*, his ethos goes well beyond food to encompass a philosophy around the role of business in society, one that is at the very heart of the emergence of commercial campaigning.

'Two hundred years ago, 85 per cent of the people on planet Earth lived on less than one dollar a day. It's business and capital that have lifted people up,' Mackey told us. 'And yet, they're not given credit for it. Businessmen are routinely stereotyped as greedy, selfish, exploiters, causing global warming, creating inequality. All the modern ills of society have been scapegoated on the capitalists . . . we have to get business people to not buy into the attacks levelled at them. They are heroic in the sense that they are the creators of prosperity, they're the ones eliminating poverty, they're the ones creating the jobs,' he says.

'A big part of what we do with conscious capitalism is show through arguments and evidence that business should embrace higher purpose. There's a better way to do business, and I think there is a movement to reform business from the inside out in terms of how it's managed [and] how it's led.'

With Whole Foods, the campaign around good food and people's lives is one that continues to grow with the business. The company offers intensive health programmes for obese or diabetic staff members and Mackey believes that the responsibility to promote healthy eating is one that business must shoulder. 'I realized how much of a responsibility we had towards the world. America is exporting our terrible food habits around the world, making other people fat and sick. Part of what I feel I want to do now [is] help educate not just our team members but the world at large.'

Mackey's standpoint and his approach to business are decidedly political: indeed the Whole Foods mission statement is codified in a document entitled the 'Declaration of Interdependence', a play on America's founding statement that reflects his company's belief in the mutually reinforcing roles of a company, its customers and stakeholders. A child of the counterculture, Mackey's campaigning urge has manifested itself in wanting to change the way the world eats and in transforming how it thinks about business, and indeed how business perceives itself. He stands for his generation of business leader: the antecedents of today's campaigning companies who continue to have a powerful voice in the debate.

Whole Foods shows that a company's ability to influence the world around it is heavily vested in its own internal sense of mission. 'Companies that have a higher sense of purpose release far more purpose, will release far more energy, far more creativity,' Mackey told us. 'Businesses need to be more successful in engaging their employees and convincing their customers that they are a place that they should be trading with ... Humans are evolving; we want to have more purpose, we want our lives to make a difference, we want to work for businesses that are more creative, and we like to think that our creativity is motivating other people.'

The idea of conscious capitalism is one that will be most commonly associated with Mackey and Whole Foods, but it is the subtitle to his book – 'Liberating the Heroic Spirit of Business' – that resonated most with us. The idea that business is a force for good, and should contribute to solving the world's problems, is at the heart of the Whole Foods story and mission.

Campaigning 2.0: the New Generation

The rise to prominence of Jobs, Branson and Mackey marked a seismic shift in the commercial landscape, the full ramifications of which we are beginning to see in today's market. What they instigated was the beginning of a gradual acceptance of entrepreneurship as a way to achieve social and economic good. Since the 1970s, the reputation of entrepreneurs has been transformed from the Del Boy and Arthur Daley wide-boy stereotypes of the 1980s to the Zuckerberg and Bezos icons of today.

This was also a generation of entrepreneurs that embodied another of the great tenets of campaigning business: communication. Jobs, Branson and Mackey may have been flower power activists on the one hand, but on the other they were accomplished, powerful and pragmatic communicators. That does not mean they were or are great orators, but rather that they had the innate and special ability to visualize a grand sweep of change, and find a way to insprie employees, customers and the market at large with its potential. They were among the first to realize that business had become a battle for attention: that words, ideas and perception are paramount in influencing people's thinking and decisions.

As children of the 1960s, they brought an overtly political approach into business: a libertarian belief in the freedom of individuals and ideas, a desire to rail against the established foundations of power and influence. Another shared trait was a very emotional connection with the businesses they created, companies powered as much by the heart as the head. 'Life is too short to do anything less than follow your heart,' Mackey told us. 'Why would you settle for anything less than that?'

Decades of technological progress may have turned the early efforts of Jobs and his ilk into museum pieces, but their establishment of a campaigning mentality at the heart of business has lived on and is central to the new generation of explosive growth companies we can now see emerging.

Needless to say, today's business landscape is vastly changed from that of the original commercial campaigners. Today's entrepreneurs operate at a time when, far from being powerless, consumers increasingly set the commercial agenda because of the platform and the voice given to them by social media.

The new generation of campaigners must be collaborative in a way their predecessors were not, and had far less need to be. While Apple undoubtedly championed choice and opportunities for the individual, its approach to product development and design has been famously dogmatic. 'A lot of times, people don't know what they want until you show it to them,' is one of Jobs' more famous sayings, reflecting a tradition of absolutist business leadership that held sway throughout much of the twentieth century, perhaps best characterized by the oft-quoted, much debated Henry Ford saying: 'If I had asked people what they wanted, they would have said faster horses.'

The campaigning businesses of today could not be more different: in constant dialogue with their customers thanks to the variety of new communications channels now available, they must embrace consumers rather than holding them at arm's-length. They see the opportunity presented by open dialogue with customers and not the threat it might pose.

In this context, the nature of mission among this generation of companies has become broader and more far-reaching, a socially driven purpose to change how people live their lives: how they eat, travel and interact. We believe these campaigners are in the vanguard of a new commercial movement, one that is harnessing technological change to create brand-new business opportunities, and winning the battle for mindshare. Next we will look at the new sectors that are emerging in a campaigner's economy and what can be learned from the businesses that represent the new generation.

Carers, Sharers and Darers

Today's commercial campaigners work in a world that is steeped in technology as never before; a world that has been the making of a generation of entrepreneurs who have anticipated and catered to new and rapidly developing consumer needs.

WANdisco's David Richards has characterized the environment in which business works today as 'dog years', with technological change happening at seven times the rate it once did. In this environment, new commercial sectors are developing. Indeed, we have observed what we believe to be three specific segments emerging from the rise of the mission-based business, the relentless pace of change and the inheritance of the entrepreneurs whose stories we tell in this book. They are:

Caring: Companies that improve people's lives;

Sharing: Companies that connect people and information;

Daring: Companies that refuse to accept no for an answer.

Companies within these categories are at the leading edge of what technology has made possible. They believe they can change the world and the way people live their lives for the better. They have added a distinctive flavour of social purpose to the disruptive, activist mentality inherited from the first generation of commercial campaigners.

Take an industry as fundamental as food. It is no secret that existing forms of food production are becoming unsustainable as the global population continues to climb. All the science suggests we cannot afford to continue to commit so much of the planet's resources to rearing the livestock that account for meat, dairy and egg production.

The answer to this environmental conundrum is starting to be cooked up in the laboratories of some of Silicon Valley's most exciting start-ups. Hampton Creek, backed by investors including Microsoft founder Bill Gates, has made a name for itself with its mission to eliminate the egg from food production and preparation. Instead, it crunches data from billions of plant proteins to determine combinations that can replace the texture and flavour an egg provides.

'About 1.8 trillion eggs are laid every year around the world, and most come from places that are destructive to the environment and pretty brutal on animals,' co-founder

Josh Tetrick told *Entrepreneur* magazine. 'We've figured out a way to make food that is better for the environment, kinder to animals and better for our bodies.'

Hampton Creek products on the market already include an eggless mayonnaise and powder to replace the need for eggs in baking, with a scrambled egg substitute set to follow. The company's website states its mission for 'everyone [to] be able to eat delicious food that's healthier, sustainable, and affordable'. In common with many disruptors, it has incited a strong response from incumbents, with Unilever filing and later withdrawing a lawsuit over the company's right to call its product mayonnaise. Controversial it may be, but as one of a rising class of Silicon Valley start-ups seeking to address the very significant challenge around how we feed the planet without destroying it, Hampton Creek stands out as an exemplar of the caring economy: a business seeking to address the health, cost and sustainability implications of its industry.

The potential impact of sharing companies is no less significant. These are the businesses harnessing the power of the Internet to create new platforms and communities that are changing the way we share information and consume goods and services.

PwC estimates the sharing economy will be worth $335 billion by 2025, and companies have sprung up allowing people to rent out everything from their home to their car and their spare time. While on a practical level these companies provide an extension of online communities into everyday life, speak to sharing economy founders and it becomes clear that their mission is around improving people's lives and how they experience the world.

Take Airbnb. The hugely successful platform for room rentals has supported more than 25 million guests since it was founded in 2008. You could easily conclude that it is little more than a well-targeted digital marketplace that has found its moment.

Yet according to co-founder Joe Gebbia, 'our brand . . . is not about accommodation, it's about belonging.'

'This is a new way of life for people,' he told us. 'We have people who will never go back to traditional accommodation. This is the future of travel, to feel again.' The online community his company has created translates into a local experience for travellers across the world. For him, Airbnb represents a fundamental break with mass-produced, identikit globetrotting, and indeed one of the most revealing parts of our interview was when he spoke of how Airbnb has allowed him to meet people and forge new relationships across the world: a new global network, the mission of business made real.

It is typical of sharing companies that they are about connecting people rather than relying on companies: a broadly shared sense of mission about a more personal, local and bespoke way of life, an antidote to anonymous, mass market consumerism. And while US companies have been in the vanguard, the sharing economy is something that has also taken root in the UK and across Europe. One of the most notable examples is BlaBlaCar, the French ride-sharing service with 20 million members across eighteen countries.

If sharing companies are, in a certain sense, about winding back the clock, the darers are fiercely future focused. These are the businesses who push the limits of what is achievable, who seek to harness the growing power of technology to achieve what would have been unimaginable feats. From drones to 3D printing, driverless cars and virtual reality, these are the businesses who believe they can change how people think, organizations work and societies function.

What unites these three types of new business is the zeal of the campaigner, and their desire to make something better. They demonstrate the very embedded sense of mission that is driving today's most successful companies: be that to make the world more sustainable, more connected or more advanced. They are not universal categories, but rather they highlight three areas in which we have observed many campaigning companies that are growing rapidly and having a major influence on the market. What follows are the stories of three businesses that highlight caring, sharing and daring at work, and the lessons you can learn from them in developing, harnessing and building your mission, and taking it forward with a campaigning approach.

Caring: Ella's Kitchen

'The idea that a business can be a force for social good is not an add-on in my business, it's a core part of business principle.' That is the view of Paul Lindley, the children's

TV executive who in 2006 founded Ella's Kitchen, now the UK's best-selling baby food provider. From day one, Ella's Kitchen was as much campaign as it was company. 'I had the idea of Ella's Kitchen as a brand before I had a clue what products we would sell, what the packaging would look like,' he says.

The idea was for a company that would change children's relationship with food. 'What drove me was the desire [to] make meaningful change to children's diets from a very young age,' Paul reflects. 'We've articulated that more concisely and more professionally as we've grown, but that is the thing that engages our team and engages the customers and suppliers that work with us . . . because there is a higher purpose.'

We have worked with Paul since 2011, including on the development of his campaigning work around childhood nutrition. He embodies the best traits of the entrepreneurial campaigner as someone who saw a serious problem in society and wanted to challenge it. Ella's Kitchen's caring credentials, as a company seeking to change the way children eat, have kept pace with its rapidly increasing sales.

'The idea for Ella's Kitchen first came around because of two strands that were happening in my life at the right time in my life. The first was personal in that I had had my first child so I was experiencing what it was like to be a parent and all the associated challenges, such as trying to feed her and feeding her the right stuff.

'The second thing was that I had been at Nickelodeon for nine years and what I'd learned there was how you can use a brand to really engage children to change their behaviour and get parents on side.'

'I had also learned about the UK's rising childhood obesity problem, and how television was being blamed for it. I could see that a third of our kids are overweight and 20 per cent of them are obese, and it was getting worse.

'I thought the biggest way we can affect and reverse those statistics and children's diets was with a business and through creating trust that comes through a business built on values. That was my driving force. I came to realize that business was the best way to try and create societal change.'

From concept to foundation, then, Ella's Kitchen has been a campaigning company that seeks to be, as its strapline reads, 'good in every sense'.

Being a caring brand, Lindley says, is at the heart of achieving commercial results that go hand-in-hand with social outcomes. 'People buy stuff because it improves their lives . . . it can improve their life functionally, it can improve their life emotionally, and if you can combine the two then you've got brand advocates and people who are passionate about what you are trying to do.

'With baby food and young children's food, you're dealing with parents who are at the most emotional part of their whole lives, so working with that emotion to provide something that improves their lives and their children's lives . . . is an open door.'

So how did Lindley go from TV executive to the boss of a thriving business? A crucial element, he told us, was to place the customer front and centre. In his case that meant understanding his buyers as parents. 'To get anywhere when our competitors are big multinationals we had to think differently, and we tried to be the people who understood what it's like to be a family in the modern world most,' he says.

'And some of that thinking is about understanding the humanness of being a parent ... an area which I don't think our competitors were particularly focused on. We've tried to communicate openly, transparently, with empathy as another person rather than a corporation to a mum or dad. On my business card, my title is Ella's Dad. As a parent to another parent, they have a reason to interact more easily with us.'

Two years ago, Paul sold Ella's Kitchen to US food company Hain Celestial. 'In looking for a partner, I wanted someone who believed in the values upon which we'd set up the business and were prepared to invest in those values and invest in the entrepreneurial thinking that we did. We found that partner in Hain Celestial. I've chosen to stay on board since the acquisition because I feel that they very much live our values and value the entrepreneurial thinking we bring to the whole group, so I don't really see a change in ownership as affecting the way in which we can develop the business.

'I don't think we've changed our brand in any significant way,' Paul reflects. 'Fundamentally it looks the same, it says the same, it's the same all-encompassing thing about improving children's relationship with food.

'We think like a human being, we think like another parent and we try within all of that to create products that they actually need, that betters their children's lives, that provides a convenient solution to improving their children's diet.'

Top Tips: Paul Lindley

1. **Values:** 'I knew the values that I brought to the business needed to survive within it, so we did practical things like getting an HR department when we only had about forty people, because we could see that the future sustainability of the brand . . . was in those values and therefore we had to codify them, ensure that they live in our culture and recruit people who believe in such values. We had to promote them and motivate the team by them, and we wanted to reward everyone based on their demonstrating those values, not just on financial performance.'

2. **Team:** 'I don't think it's an accident that we find ourselves as sixty-five people, 75 per cent of whom are women, 50 per cent of whom are parents and about 25 per cent of whom are part-time or flexible working people. Because all those three groups are interested in our brand and our product, because it fits with their life interests and we can build their job around their needs as well as our needs.'

3. **Brand:** 'Brands are so important because people aren't just logical robots. We're people with emotions

and we think illogically sometimes, we go with our hearts sometimes and we rely a lot on trust. Trust is central to our lives and good brands recognize that and build their businesses around gaining and retaining such trust. That is what I tried to set out for from the beginning.'

Sharing: Airbnb

When Airbnb founders Brian Chesky and Joe Gebbia started their business – now valued at over $13 billion – it could hardly have looked less like a world-beater.

The two college friends had quit their jobs to work together and Chesky put his life's belongings in the back of his car to join Gebbia in San Francisco.

The problem? His starting fund was $1,000; the monthly rent $1,150. Then came the idea that started it all. An international design conference was coming to town that weekend, with hotels block-booked. The pair struck on the notion of renting out space in their apartment, as a bed and breakfast. Except the only beds they could offer were air mattresses. Hence, Air Bed and Breakfast was born, a website was rustled up in twenty-four hours and the first three paying guests arrived. Twenty-five million would follow in the next six years.

'It was not a start-up, it was a way for us to make rent,' Chesky recalled in a 2011 interview with tech publication GigaOM. 'We thought the idea was absurd, ourselves, and I think a lot of my friends did too. We thought it was just a way to make rent and then we decided we'd keep doing it as a way to keep making rent until we came up with the idea [for the business]. We didn't think this was the idea.'

Today, Airbnb has evolved well beyond a marketplace for spare beds, rooms and floors. It is, as Chesky has described it, 'a community marketplace where you can book anything from a private apartment to a private island.' Other listed abodes include an igloo ($267 a night), castle ($133) and family treehouse (complete with a six-month waiting list).

It was a combination of good luck and good judgment that saw the concept begin to take flight. In 2009, Airbnb was accepted by famed Silicon Valley start-up school Y Combinator. The founders were fine-tuning the service through first-hand experience, staying in Airbnb rooms across New York on their weekends. In March 2009, venture investment arrived from Sequoia Capital, backers of Google, YouTube and any number of tech success stories.

Gradually, the sharing bug started to bite. In Gebbia's words, 'It's this social connection, connecting with the person and their spaces. It's about real spaces and real people. This is what we never anticipated but this has been the secret sauce behind Airbnb.'

It is this very personal element that has helped turn the company into a remarkable brand, one that is increasingly becoming an everyday part of booking holidays and accommodation. 'People appreciate the humanity of the service,' Gebbia told us. 'They don't feel like a number, they feel like a name. It's about the warmth of the home, we fulfill an emotional need.'

He has hosted over 250 guests at his own home and talks about having made friends from around the world. 'No matter where you are, there is this spirit that you can belong anywhere in the world, by being part of a community when you are travelling.'

And that belonging is in becoming a producer as much as a consumer. 'We used to live in a world where there [were] people, private citizens, a world where there [were] businesses, and now we're living in a world where people can become businesses in sixty seconds,' Chesky told the Aspen Ideas Festival in 2013. He estimates that the sharing economy will create over 100 million micro-entrepreneurs on the Airbnb model.

As he put it to the *Wall Street Journal* in 2014, 'There were laws created for businesses and there were laws for people. What the sharing economy did was to create a third category: people as businesses.' Indeed, Airbnb has grown to such an extent that it has spawned its own start-up ecosystem, of companies that handle and vet bookings for busy users sometimes overwhelmed by the demand on their properties.

According to its founder, the sharing pioneers are not just providing a basis for people to get more from their assets, but a passport into a more social, choice-rich world. 'The more you broadcast your reputation, the more you'll have access to. You can decide to live off the grid, not have a reputation, and that's fine ... But, fewer people will know you and you'll have access to fewer things.'

From renting out their own living room to changing how millions view their property and privacy, Airbnb has come an unthinkably long way in such a short time. An everyday problem shared with the world has become a multi-billion dollar market.

Above all, the lesson it teaches is that you don't have to be a fully formed, serial entrepreneur to make it big. The Airbnb story shows that the opportunity for entrepreneurs is universal, and that the campaigning ethos is not something that will necessarily be there on the first day of trading, but which may very well emerge and develop at the pace of your business, as can your mission.

Top Tips: Airbnb

1. **Stay the course:** 'It took about a year to get 100 users. And now we get that in an hour,' Brian Chesky has said. 'No one wanted to be the first person to do this. It's one of those concepts that, once it gets going, everyone wants to do it, but no one wants to be the first to try it.' The lesson? Even the best ideas can take time to catch on. Don't be disheartened if you don't hit an immediate home run.

2. **Opportunism:** During the 2008 Democratic National Convention (DNC), with Obamania at its height, the Airbnb founders took advantage of a chronic problem of supply: 'All the hotels in Denver were sold out so

we had this idea,' Chesky later recalled. 'What if we got Obama supporters to open up their homes to other Obama supporters?'

The lack of accommodation had become a news story and Air Bed and Breakfast got its first national awareness as a grass-roots alternative. 'We went from three guys working out of a living room with no money, to three guys working out of a living room with no money, but we had a ton of press,' Joe Gebbia said in 2013.

3. **Be inventive:** After the bounce in interest following the DNC came the slump and Airbnb looked like it was back where it had started. Then the founders hit on what must rank as one of the most novel start-up fundraising ploys you could wish to hear. The idea was a branded breakfast product that could be mailed to Airbnb's hosts as part of the service.

   The result had the unmistakable tinge of 'yes we can': a breakfast cereal for both presidential nominees, 'Obama-O's (hope in every bowl) and Cap'n McCain's (a maverick in every bite). And from there, as Chesky later recalled, 'we funded our company by creating cereal.' More specifically, by repackaging shop-bought cereal in the unique boxes, which sold at $40 a time to bring in over $20,000.

Daring: Uber

It has been named one of America's most hated companies, received a torrent of cease-and-desist court orders, and incited protest and gridlock in capitals across Europe. It's also the company considered to be the world's most valuable start-up, with an estimated – and much debated – $40-billion price tag.

Taxi app Uber is the company that everyone has an opinion on: from its 8 million global subscribers to the taxi industry, which calls it illegal, the municipal authorities (from New Delhi to Frankfurt) who have banned it, and the investors who have stumped up a collective $4.9 billion to fund the company since its launch in 2010. One of the simplest executions of the on-demand economy – tapping a button to summon a nearby cab – has also become one of the most contested business models of recent years.

'We are running a political campaign and the candidate is Uber,' co-founder Travis Kalanick has frequently said. The company demonstrably recognizes that the battle it faces is for more than just market share. The Uber senior team now includes David Plouffe, who led Barack Obama's 2008 presidential campaign; it has commissioned research into its economic model from another former Obama aide, economist Alan Krueger.

The convergence of top Washington political talent with deep-pocketed West Coast investors highlights how Uber is working to build something broader than a business, and to punch harder than any traditional lobbying campaign. Past the noise, the controversies and the rapid growth in customer and driver numbers, Uber is seeking something beyond the fundamentals of commercial success. Instead, as is amply evidenced by the furious outcry from its incumbents, Uber is trying to change the structure of the urban transport market.

'Transportation as reliable as running water everywhere and for everyone.' That is how Uber sums up its mission. In its first five years, its progress towards that aim has been rapid, to say the least. Every day, an estimated one million rides are being taken in Uber cabs across the world, with the company's approximately 160,000 registered drivers, across 290 cities. In San Francisco, where the service first launched, Uber's annual revenues are $500 million, more than three times the size of the city's taxi market. Similarly, there are now more Uber cars on the road in New York than iconic yellow cabs.

Such rates of consumer adoption and revenue growth are enough in themselves to set the company apart. Yet where Uber epitomizes the new generation of daring technology companies is less in what it has done already than what it ultimately seeks to achieve. That is a fundamental shift in how people travel and cities function. In London, its goal is to take a million cars off the road by 2020 through the UberPool ride-sharing service, addressing not just the immediate consumer need but the wider social problem of congestion and air quality. Another 2020 ambition it has expressed is to recruit a million women drivers, against the historic gender imbalance of the industry. Uber has argued for its service and the ride-sharing model as a solution for everything from city congestion to drink driving, claiming that its entry into Seattle helped bring about a 10 per cent reduction in driving-under-the-influence arrests.

From the London standpoint, the emergence of Uber as a genuine disruptor has been highly visible, most of all when the capital's black cab drivers blockaded central London in protest against the city's refusal to regulate against Uber drivers. An 850 per cent increase in London registrations to Uber was the result, and the very public battle between challenger and incumbent created a powerful platform for the company. Time will tell how serious Uber is in its stated aim to take a million cars off London's roads, but its willingness to tackle congestion, one of the city's major issues, is a good indication of a mission-based business at work.

The other major, and much debated, aspect of the Uber story is the people who make the service possible: its drivers. Opposing poles of opinion hold that the company is either empowering or risks impoverishing the people who ferry its customers around the world's cities. Across the spectrum, stories diverge between drivers reporting they make less than the minimum wage, and others who speak about the flexibility and self-employment opportunity that the platform has offered them. Our own experience, on a visit to the States, was that many Uber drivers were using it as an opportunity to raise money to fund other ambitions, including new start-ups. While that will not be the universal experience, what cannot be denied is that Uber is at the heart of deep-rooted change within the labour market, where individuals' ability to set their own terms of employment, as freelance contractors, is on the rise. It has created its own tribe, a platform bringing people together and creating a strong degree of empowerment.

The criticisms will continue but so, it seems, will Uber and its unerring appetite for expansion, big-ticket ambition and, one might even argue, controversy. At its San Francisco headquarters, the conference centre is a self-styled 'War Room', which captures the mentality of a business ready to take on all comers, and which has freely talked about its attempts to sabotage the fundraising of one competitor, Lyft. Its founder, the *Financial Times* has written, is 'one of Silicon Valley's toughest fighters, with an unusual ability to convince others to join him in taking on the world, and a fierceness developed over more than a decade spent fighting to make it as an entrepreneur.' Kalanick has described himself as 'a passionate entrepreneur . . . like fire and brimstone sometimes'.

Still a young company, Uber is defined by the daring mentality that allows it to believe it can change the way the world moves. In just five years, it has already done much to suggest that belief has evolved from a prideful notion to a realizable ambition. It shows the way forward for how daring technology can make a fast and real difference in today's society.

Top Tips: Uber

1. **Persistence pays:** Uber is not Travis Kalanick's first business but his third. He was not the precocious Young Turk of Valley legend when he created it, but in his thirties with one failed and one moderate business behind him. Indeed, the story of the company's creation holds that he seriously questioned his own desire to try his hand at entrepreneurship again before agreeing to go into business with co-founder Garrett Camp. 'The reason he is who he is, is because he failed twice,' one insider has been quoted on Kalanick. The lesson? Persistence pays in the quest for business success.

2. **Stick to your guns:** Looking to close one of Uber's many funding rounds in October 2011, Kalanick became stuck in negotations with Andreessen Horowitz, one of Silicon Valley's most renowned funds. He eventually turned down a rich counter-offer which fell below his own valuation: a big risk for a company only in its second year, but one which in retrospect has left most observers to suggest it was Andreesen Horowitz that had missed the big opportunity.

3. **Go big or go home:** Big ideas and bold ambitions have been a defining part of the Uber story. 'Kalanick's vision is much more than a better taxi service or nifty

town cars for the masses,' *Vanity Fair* has written.
'He sees in Uber the potential for a smoothly
functioning instant-gratification economy, powered
by the smartphone as the remote control for life.'
From a million cars off the road in London by 2020 to
a million more women drivers, Uber has never been
afraid to set out its stall. Its scale and reach may be
that much greater than the vast majority of
companies, but the lesson that vision and ambition
precedes delivery is an important one, however big
or small the business.

The Campaigning Legacy

As the above stories have sought to demonstrate, it is a
campaigning mentality that underpins some of the most
successful companies in today's marketplace. While this
was captured by a cluster of 1970s and 1980s companies
who presented themselves as an antidote to the forces of
the corporate world, it has been taken forward by a generation of businesses whose mission is fundamentally about
a better existence for people and the planet.

That may seem like a daunting ask for an entrepreneur
just starting out. And not every company can or will be
about changing the world. Nor will all missions emerge
fully formed as the business is founded. Contrast Ella's
Kitchen, a company built around a social purpose, with
Airbnb, a quick-fix which caught on and has developed a

campaigning mentality, and Uber, where an idea built around convenience has evolved into a much broader piece about the future of cities and travel.

But the point to take is that these companies have prospered through a very conscious outlook on what they wanted to be and how they could make a difference to their market. That mission, and the campaigning flair with which they have brought it to life, is something that can be emulated by any business in any field. If you can't answer the questions about why your proposition is different, what consumer or market need it addresses or how you can attract customers, then it's time to pause and think again.

In today's market, the pace of change means that success is nearer the reach of new companies than ever before. Indeed, what is notable about the contemporary economy is the prevalence of high-growth businesses and the pace with which they scale. That is the subject of our next chapter: the momentum that is parachuting emerging start-ups into the commercial stratosphere.

Takeaways

- A mission is nothing without a campaigner and a campaigning team to make it real. A campaigner must embody the activist mentality, optimistic in their belief that they – and their followers – can change business, and society, for the better;

- Today's campaigning attitude towards business has its origins in the rebellious entrepreneurial stance born out of the social upheaval of the 1960s that helped define the original activist campaigner who has become the hero of today's entrepreneurs;
- Out of the new economy have arisen three different types of campaigning companies who have created their own markets. These are the Carers – companies that improve people's lives; the Sharers – companies that bring people together; and the Darers – companies that refuse to take no for an answer;
- The founders of the new generation of campaigning businesses like Airbnb, Ella's Kitchen and Uber, were unafraid to challenge the corporate giants that dominate their respective industries. They share a fearlessness in taking on the status quo.

3

Momentum

Nothing happens until something moves.
Albert Einstein

We believe that great businesses start with mission and achieve scale through campaigning. But these are not easy things to track or quantify. The measure of success, the hallmark of successful companies, is momentum. The greatest prize has become less market share and more speed of progression. The smart money is on the agile fast-mover over the immobile incumbent. This chapter will examine how some of the notable Internet-era companies have turned mission into momentum.

Momentum has become critical in a world where the cycle of business boom and bust has become shorter than ever before, and companies that are not coming up will often be crashing down. It is perhaps easier to recognize than to define; indeed, just as many have often called reputation the 'Cinderella asset', something whose worth is only truly acknowledged once it has been lost – the same could be said of momentum. But make no mistake, when a business has momentum – that ineffable sense of movement – it can seem unstoppable. For a small company it allows you to transcend the limitations of your size and scope; for the big beasts, negative momentum is something that everything must be geared to avoiding. Just as political candidates have become accustomed to laser-like scrutiny on their opinions, behaviour and public pronouncements, so too business leaders are increasingly faced with heightened levels of public critique and challenge.

That is true across all sectors and industries: the rise and rise of the Internet has meant fundamental change across the board. But for some the upheaval has been more violent and potentially terminal than others.

Take the news media. You do not have to go far to find the obituaries being written for traditional publications: the American Enterprise Institute found in 2013 that advertising revenues for US newspapers had fallen to their lowest level since the 1950s, once adjusted for inflation. The demise, from a peak of $65.8 billion at the turn of the millennium, to approximately $17 billion in 2013, is akin to a sustained stock market slump when plotted on a graph.

As the fortunes of established media brands wane, with some notable exceptions, a rapid emergence of digital outlets has been widely credited with changing the news landscape. BuzzFeed, founded in 2006, reaches over 150 million unique viewers monthly, compared to 57 million for *The New York Times* or 31 million for the *Wall Street Journal* online.

Last year, BuzzFeed secured $50 million of venture capital funding in a deal that valued the company at

$850 million, where the *Washington Post* was deemed worthy of only a $250 million price tag when purchased by Amazon founder Jeff Bezos in 2013.

That is still less than half the market cap of *The New York Times*, which hovered around the $2 billion mark in late 2014. Yet the most important part of the BuzzFeed story is not absolute market position compared to traditional competitors, but its speed of growth. The 'paper of record' has seen more wiped off its valuation than BuzzFeed is currently worth in total, just in the six years since the challenger was founded.

BuzzFeed is without question a brand with momentum, a rapid mover in a sector where explosive growth sits side by side with seemingly irreversible decline. At the end of 2013, CNN was able to declare that its digital arm had enjoyed 'the best year in its history'. Its 67 million average monthly viewers represented a 9 per cent year-on-year increase in unique users. The equivalent figure for Buzz-Feed, contrasting November 2013 with the previous year, was a 350 per cent surge.

That is a momentum built on a clear and defined sense of mission, which can be seen from a memo sent by founder Jonah Peretti, also co-founder of the Huffington Post, to staff in August 2014. 'We are building the defining news and entertainment company for the social, mobile age.' Beyond that, as he told *Wired* last year, BuzzFeed has been defined against the gossip-fuelled negativity of much early digital media: 'There was an era when snarking was what blogs did. On the social web it's about building a larger society.'

Its momentum is evident in far more than just its viewer numbers and company value. Look at its people: in the last two to three years, a steady stream of high-profile journalists from hallmark print publications has moved over to the land of lists and llamas. The BuzzFeed staff is now replete with Pulitzer Prize winners, former *New York Times* editors and, in the UK, senior staffers from publications including the *Daily Telegraph*, the *Guardian*, *The Times* and the *Sun*.

The idea that an established journalist would leave a mainstream national title for a nascent online operation would have been curious five years ago, and considered akin to career suicide a decade ago. Yet now it has become not just a workable option, but in many cases a desirable one. That is the power of momentum at work: a rising force that, even in relative infancy, is too interesting and attractive to turn down. This is the greatest and surest measure of success in a fast-moving and unstable environment for business. Not market incumbency, which increasingly presents as many threats to mega-brands as it does benefits, but the lure that surrounds a company on the rise: creating something new, progressing at pace and attracting in people who will bring others with them in turn. 'There is no deodorant like success', the Hollywood star Elizabeth Taylor once commented. And in today's market, it is companies in the first flush of their success that are often the most appealing. They have the momentum that builds followings and can turn a big idea into a powerful reality.

The 'Big Mo'

Momentum is a concept most immediately recognizable in the sporting and political arenas, particularly in the US, where 'the Big Mo' is a fixed part of the narrative of election campaigns. And just as today's business leaders have much to learn from the arts of the electioneer, so too can they benefit from how politicians measure their impact and survey for pitfalls.

Former Havas CEO David Jones talks about how he appropriated lessons from the political world, by encouraging brands to think like candidates running for election. Principally, he worked on momentum polling, looking at whether a brand was rising or falling in the market, with the degree of movement much more significant than the absolute market position.

Momentum has become such an important measure of success for companies because of the growing pace of change that surrounds business. In a denser, more competitive and unstable marketplace, market positions can be wiped out at great speed and it is more dangerous than ever to take your success for granted.

Destabilizing threats abound, most tangibly in the form of new entrants and innovators, ready to eat your lunch at a moment's notice. In this landscape the ability to keep moving forward becomes paramount: the avoidance of stagnation or the impression that you have fallen into, or indeed behind, the crowd matters more than ever before.

Just as politicians must keep a constant gauge on the

news cycle and emerging opportunities and threats, so too is business now bound to the constant feedback loop of digital and social media. Increasingly, business is subject to the same level of threat and challenge as politicians have long been accustomed to: what start out as small issues in a far-off country of which we know little can quickly mushroom into a crisis that threatens reputation and market capitalization.

And it is not just the choppy waters of new media and customer opinion that companies must now learn to navigate. With influential companies growing in greater numbers and more quickly than ever, the threat of being outpaced by a new competitor is a constant and not a periodic one.

It is in the search for momentum that businesses can find the urgency needed to prosper in a demanding and competitive marketplace. Measuring your success more often, and relative to your marketplace, allows you to keep a closer handle on imminent threats and competitor developments.

Momentum is something all companies crave, although it is more symptom than root cause of success. What it offers is a means of tracking success in an unpredictable market and a pertinent question for any business owner or manager to ask themselves: are we moving forward or standing still? Are our competitors ahead of us or behind? The mentality of a constant election cycle will enable businesses to ensure they are consistently meeting customer needs, keeping pace with competitors and anticipating decisive new trends. If business can learn one thing from the political arena, it is that you can never really stop moving if you want to stay ahead.

Equal and Opposite Reactions

If forward momentum is an unstoppable force powering some companies to great heights in next to no time, then the opposite experience can be equally rapid and vigorous. Today's business market has the capacity to chew up and spit out even those companies whose market position seems unassailable, once a downward spiral of negative momentum gathers force.

In some cases, a falling giant and rising star will coincide, with one prescient case being that of video rental behemoth Blockbuster and on-demand video pioneer Netflix. When the latter was founded in 1997 as a DVD postal service, Blockbuster controlled approximately a quarter of the $16-billion home video rental market.

Three years later, Netflix founder Reed Hastings flew to Dallas to meet Blockbuster's chief executive John Antioco. The offer he tabled was to sell a 49 per cent stake in Netflix for $50 million and to operate as the high street giant's online arm.

The discussions did not progress and, without the benefit of hindsight, the reasons seem eminently logical. Netflix had only 300,000 subscribers and was losing money. Blockbuster was valued at around $3 billion, with a global network of over 8,000 stores, which would grow to in excess of 9,000 by 2004, when the company employed as many as 60,000.

Yet five years on, those 300,000 had increased to 3.4 million subscribers and Netflix was spreading its wings in the online market, one Blockbuster had belatedly entered in 2004, spending hundreds of millions playing catch-up. When it finally went bankrupt in 2010, a year in which it lost $1.1 billion, the tables had more than turned from the meeting a decade earlier: stricken Blockbuster valued at $24 million and Netflix a towering $13 billion. Across a ten-year period, a household name had been turned to dust, while a little-known upstart grew into one of the showcase brands of the Internet era. It is an extreme example of the momentum that a small business can create around a major market opportunity such as the shift to digital video: not just supercharging its own prospects but effectively putting out of business a brand that once looked too big to fail.

While Netflix was a natural beneficiary of the Internet era, as an agile, low-cost start-up against Blockbuster's legacy infrastructure and high overheads, it also made the difficult decisions that its competitor refused to, showing a willingness to disrupt its own business model to keep pace with market developments and build towards its mission to be the world's leading entertainment channel in a society that leaves traditional television behind altogether. Pivoting from DVD rentals to online streaming in 2007 unlocked a burgeoning market which now sees the website account for a staggering 35 per cent of bandwidth usage in North America (against 14 per cent for YouTube and under 3 per cent for Facebook). It was the combination of vision and willingness to pursue the new opportunity that allowed Netflix to maintain its momentum, even as the business model that had brought its initial successes was running out of road.

Harnessing Momentum

Momentum, then, is perhaps the greatest of all intangible business assets, the hallmark of today's commercial winners.

There is a certain irrepressible quality to momentum brands: those whose ideas and execution capture the perfect moment of opportunity in their market. That is not something which will often happen immediately or even quickly. Recall the long, hard yards undertaken by the Airbnb founders at a time when their idea had anything but momentum. Yet the accumulation of users and the inherent shareability of the concept soon delivered a noticeable effect.

'At some point the flywheel gets going,' founder Brian Chesky has said. 'We're an international site, there's people going from one city to another on our website. And by doing that they're spreading the concept. People will come from all over the world to San Francisco and then take the concept back to where they've come from. There's a natural network effect that's built in.'

In other words, the community and network that Airbnb

developed fed itself into exponential growth, soon putting gale-force winds in the sails of the brand, from what seemed a slow starting point.

Momentum is not something that can be easily quantified, bottled or attained. But that does not mean that you should treat it as an abstract measure of success and nothing more.

While in your own business it is something that will be obtained through the right combination of opportunism and good fortune, momentum can act as your roadmap for the wider market, helping to spot the trends before they happen and dodge the punches before they land.

David Jones told us how the advertising group Havas developed the Brand Momentum barometer as a means of predicting how markets would move and fortunes would wax and wane. 'We did [momentum polling] at Havas in 2004, way before Google was what it has become today,' he said. 'Then AOL was number one and Google was number eleven. But ask the question on momentum, AOL had massively negative momentum and Google had all the momentum. It absolutely predicted what was going to happen in the future.' Examining momentum over absolute market position, he says, 'gives you a level of insight and knowledge that is so much sharper and finer'.

Mapping trends to try and predict how a market will develop may not always be possible or even accurate. But the state of mind that momentum polling encourages – a rigorous focus on the wider market, changes and emerging powers – is what every company can learn from and put into practice. Ultimately the businesses with momentum are those who have, by whatever combination of luck and judgment, happened upon the right idea at the right time. You significantly increase the judgment element with a consistent and smart landscaping of your market. If yours is the business which can see the waves before they crash down, as Netflix did and Blockbuster so comprehensively did not, then you give yourself the best possible chance of building the momentum that will supercharge every conceivable element of the business.

Takeaways

- It is companies with momentum rather than market position who thrive in today's landscape: speed of movement should be prized over strength of incumbency;
- The past decade has seen iconic companies across a number of industries felled by their lack of momentum relative to young, start-up competitors;
- Momentum is the symptom and not the cause of success, but it is the yardstick business owners must constantly measure themselves by: are we moving forwards or falling back?
- By focusing your market research on momentum trends, you stand a better chance of harnessing major changes as they happen, and leading rather than following the market.

4

Becoming a Campaigner

Attitude is a little thing that makes a big difference.
Winston Churchill

The journey from mission to momentum is not one that every business will succeed in making. Indeed, as we will go on to explore, failure can be an essential prerequisite to long-term success. Companies that do break through are invariably led and staffed by people who are themselves fiercely motivated, who act as campaigners in their own right.

These businesses attain the air of exceptionalism, but it was not always so. We asked Whole Foods founder John Mackey if he always knew he could build a world-beater. 'Of course not,' he shot back. 'I would have been a complete megalomaniac to think that, aged twenty-five.'

The point is a serious one. Companies with multi-billion dollar valuations like Airbnb and Dropbox at first glance seem in a completely different universe to most people starting out at their kitchen table. But it bears remembering that just seven years ago, Airbnb was two friends who couldn't afford to pay their rent. Today, YouTube is a constant companion for billions of people around the world but it barely existed just ten years ago.

In our quickening economy, almost anything is possible when the right person collides with the right idea at the right time. Inspiration and opportunity are two of the prerequisites to business success. But you also need to embody certain characteristics, all of which can be acquired and developed. We have identified seven traits of an effective campaigner so that you can learn from their behaviours, whether as an aspiring entrepreneur or someone who wants to inject some of their spark into a corporate career.

These traits are drive, self-improvement, communication, disruption, persuasion, connection and optimism. You may already possess one or some of these characteristics but now is the time to fill in the missing gaps. And remember, all campaigners have to start small but it is these characteristics that get them off the starting block in the first place.

One: Drive (Or the Refusal to Give In)

The Roman military writer Renatus states that: 'In a time of peace prepare for war.' The point underpins a central characteristic of the campaigner: relentless drive. It's not over until I say it is. This unerring focus on success, all costs, the quest for the deal and the ability to negotiate until the end are all at the heart of what drives the campaigner forward.

As Dale Carnegie wrote in *How to Win Friends and Influence People*, 'Even in such technical lines as engineering, about 15 per cent of one's financial success is due to one's technical knowledge and about 85 per cent is due to skill in human engineering, to personality and the ability to lead people.'

We believe that what makes a great many campaigners powerful is their ability to lead. It demonstrates decisiveness, builds a following, and propels you to meet people and make connections.

Drive means taking the meeting that looks unpromising but brings an unlikely opportunity. It means refusing to listen to all the people telling you that the big idea is unattainable. It means going the extra mile to do a great job when a good one would do.

Sport is often a world where you see drive come to life in a very visible way. But it's more than just performance, it's about state of mind. The basketball legend turned entrepreneur, Michael Jordan, captured that when he said: 'I can accept failure, everyone fails at something. But I can't accept not trying.'

That is a mantra for campaigners to live by and something to look for in your team: people who, to stick with the sporting analogy, convert the half-chances. Who apply themselves to the greatest challenges with a determination to succeed whatever the circumstances.

According to Kate Robertson, co-founder of international youth movement One Young World, 'you absolutely need the obsession [to campaign]. I think 90 per cent of the time people don't agree with you and you are getting steamrollered, so you need that. With a small "r" it becomes a religion: you are pushing water uphill and you just have to keep doing it.'

Two: Self-improvement

During our first five years in business, one of the big debates has been about whether entrepreneurs are born or made. What seems increasingly clear is that many of the attributes that make up the successful founder can be taught and learned. It's why the phrase 'put that down to experience' works so well. It implies the positive effects of learning and it is an integral part of the entrepreneur experience.

Cobra beer founder Lord Bilimoria often says that: 'Good judgment comes from experience; and experience comes from bad judgment.'

No doubt, it is exciting to make the point that success boils down to the hunger and passion that you are born with. But its bedfellow is being smart, and that is why many of the great entrepreneurs have always been sponges for knowledge because it gets them ahead of the pack.

When Henry Dimbleby and John Vincent founded their restaurant chain Leon, for example, one of the first things they did was to spend a month working at Burger

King, in order to learn the ropes of how a fast food restaurant worked at first hand. When they realized on opening their first restaurant that the menu wasn't right, they took a pair of scissors to it without a moment's hesitation.

When John Mackey founded Whole Foods, it took him a while to hit on his winning formula: from starting with $45,000, he ended the first year making a loss of $23,000 and a profit of only $5,000 in year two. Passion alone was not enough: Mackey, who had no prior business background, read book after book to educate himself and to come up with his formula about business. Later, when Whole Foods' buying policy was criticized by author Michael Pollan, Mackey debated him publicly: realizing the author was right on certain issues, he changed the company's policy accordingly.

A good campaigner is one who isn't afraid to learn, both through educating themselves, and through experience. Let's leave it with Voltaire, who put all this another way: 'Originality is nothing but judicious imitation.' It's a learned lesson that has made the fortune of many campaigners.

Three: Communication

Great campaigners are without exception great communicators. Getting your message across to a whole variety of people – from prospective customers to employees, investors and critics – is the foundation of good business in today's information-rich, attention-poor market.

Without communication there can be no campaign: no

supporters recruited, no advocates enlisted, no audiences persuaded. Communication is the first step to bringing an idea into reality: turning the germ of possibility into something that people want to buy or be a part of. By communication, we mean more than the ability to speak well in public. Some of the greatest business communicators may have been considered indifferent orators, but their ability to visualize and convey the big idea is what set them apart.

Communication creates the promise that captures attention and makes people want to buy or invest in you. Leon's John Vincent put it to us like this: 'By communicating better, organizations and people become better . . . and by explaining a vision more clearly, people are more likely to make that a reality. The most effective organizations put communication at the centre of what they do.'

Some in business, particularly in more traditional corporate boardrooms, have tended to dismiss communication and consider it a minor matter to be sub-contracted to the PR and marketing function. In today's market, where reputation is a live asset on which a company trades on a daily basis, that is just not good enough.

The battleground has moved from what you do to what people say, think and feel about you. This is the battle for reputation, it's a battle for the mind, and communication is the best tool in your armoury.

And if clear and open communication is your protection against threats to corporate reputation, it is also an important tool in growth and development. Campaigners are defined by the constant urge to innovate, progress and gain momentum and are equally likely to become frustrated when they cannot deliver against this need.

We have advised clients with highly successful businesses who have bemoaned just such an inability to get their machine marching in step with their ambitions. Often the problem will be one of unclear communication. If the intent has not been clearly stated both to the team and the external market, it follows that delivery is likely to be equally confused and uncertain.

Great campaigners leave no one in any doubt about what they are seeking to achieve and by what means. Through clear communication they carve out a path that allows the rest to follow.

Four: Disruption

Any young student who has been described as a 'disruptive influence' in a school report will tell you that it was hardly a comment that helped make their academic career. Describe an entrepreneur in the same way and it is a badge of honour and a symbol of business success. Disruption in business means challenging the status quo: creating opportunities and exerting influence.

So on the one hand, society does its best to fit square pegs into round holes in younger life, while at the same time championing those same alleged sins later on. It's a curious state of affairs and one that each new generation of entrepreneurs has to fight against, to keep their instincts in check when schooling is advocating the very opposite.

Someone who was considered disruptive at school would be considered a leader as a campaigner.

Someone who was dismissed as a daydreamer would in the business world be hailed a visionary.

Someone constantly distracted in lessons would find their restlessness being perceived as a symbol of their creativity.

Someone whose school career was marked down for stubbornness would be hailed by fellow entrepreneurs as having the single-minded determination to succeed.

For those who can hold on to their instincts, the rewards are immense. Joe Cohen was fired from his first job at sixteen for 'lacking initiative' and went on to found Seatwave, the secondary ticket market website that allows fans to buy unwanted tickets safely and securely. He believes disruption and entrepreneurship go hand in hand:

'I've always had problems with authority in my life. I was a poor student. I never finished university. I just wanted to get on and do stuff . . . the people who have the "right stuff" to be successful generally have an idea or a spark to do something different, do something for themselves.'

Then there's Wilfred Emmanuel-Jones, who launched his Black Farmer range of sausages in 2004. For him, being disruptive was a key factor for his business: 'Everything about my brand is about disruption. You need to be a disruptive type to be an entrepreneur, to take personal responsibility and give it a go. You need to be a bit of an upstart, a nuisance and maybe even disliked. And you will find a tipping point when you are listened to.'

Five: Persuasion

When Will King launched his King of Shaves brand of shaving oils in 1993, he wanted Harrods to be his first customer. The problem was, despite frequently sending the grooming and toiletries buyer his samples, he couldn't get an answer.

King learned the Harrods switchboard number by heart as he rang again and again for a response: 'I'd repeatedly get her assistant, who'd say: "It's on her desk, she'll be looking at it shortly", or "Yes, she's looked at it and is going to get back to you soon."'

The trouble was, she never did. Eventually, King decided to take a gamble. He rang up the private office of Mohamed Al-Fayed (the owner of Harrods) to explain the situation and asked if he could fax the details about the product to him direct.

King faxed over the details. The next morning, there was a fax waiting for him in the spare bedroom that was doubling up as his office: Harrods had placed an order for twenty-five bottles. It was the company's first order.

When you launch a business, particularly in the start-up phase, you rarely have more than the force of belief and ideas to power you. With it you get your first taste of influence, the ability to persuade – from your first hire having the belief to join you to your first client having the trust to give you a go.

It is the ability to persuade that helps you survive in the early days when your collateral assets are weak and your track record is non-existent. You must be at your peak as a salesman for your brand and vision, projecting an image not of what you are (a starter office, few or no employees, little in the way of track record) but what you want to become.

Persuasion is what wins the crucial first steps – the first piece of business, the first staff member, the first investor – from which the rest can then follow.

Six: Connection

After persuasion comes connection. In this regard entrepreneurship leaves you with no fallback position. You have no option but to go out and make your name and one for your business. Your livelihood and that of the people you employ depend on it.

'The era of traditional, top-down power is over,' said *GQ* editor Dylan Jones when announcing the magazine's inaugural list of the UK's 100 Most Connected Men, in which we featured. 'Connection is the new influence, and today's achievers operate via a free-flowing exchange of ideas, using social media and personal networks to create value and understanding.'

One of the business world's most famous networkers is the Huffington Post founder Arianna Huffington. An asset she carefully built up in the years prior to the launch of her media company was the contacts book. Her socializing skills are legendary: according to TV host Bill Maher, 'If Arianna wants to be your friend, I mean, give up. You're like a weak swimmer in a strong tide.'

What this meant was that Huffington had the great and the good to call on to write guest articles for her: Barack Obama, Hillary Clinton, Madonna and Robert Redford are just some of the many famous names who have written for the site over the years.

Of course not everyone can have the White House on call, but nor is it true that you can inherently lack the contacts or the wherewithal to get your name out there. The opportunities for networking and building a black book are more open and available than ever, and in the early stages of building a business you need a relentless focus on getting out, meeting people and making connections. And you would be surprised at how quickly your network can grow: when the technology investor Russ Shaw founded campaign group Tech London Advocates in 2013, he had a membership of 150 founders, CEOs and investors. Within two years, that number was over a thousand, demonstrating how a brand can rapidly build momentum and support with the right approach to networking and a willingness to make new connections.

It may not immediately convert and we have won contracts in some cases years after first getting to know the people. But if you are not establishing a base of connections and gaining valuable recognition and word-of-mouth support, your campaign faces being stopped dead in its tracks. So remember to take time to put aside the paperwork, difficult as it may seem, and to accept that party invitation. Or better still, throw your own.

Seven: Optimism

In all campaigning companies, but particularly those in the technology sector, you need a healthy slug of optimism to immunize yourself against the criticisms and setbacks that will inevitably come your way.

Campaigners are fixated with confronting the impossible at every turn. From technology-led cancer cures through DNA coding to realizing the potential of big data, there is an impatience to make the impossible not only realizable but inevitable. It's not bragging, it's just part of living in an intense world that is limitless in its scope and ambition.

Many entrepreneurs we know and work with could be characterized as pathological optimists: people agitated by the status quo, restless for change and haunted by the idea of missed opportunities. That is necessary because so often the first incarnation of a new idea with potential will be ruthlessly shot down by everyone except its creators.

Take Sarah Wood, co-founder of adtech company Unruly, who, not content with being the market leader in getting videos shared online, decided to take on the task of predicting the success of content that had yet to be aired.

'All our clients said it wasn't possible, any journalist we talked to said that's not possible. People within the company said it wasn't possible. And me, Matt [Cooke] and Scott [Button, the co-founders] said actually, we think it is possible.'

That belief was what led to ShareRank, the algorithm that predicts the future for video, telling brands how successful their advert will be. 'We can predict, with 80 per cent success, the share rate, the reasons people are going to share it, the places they are going to share it and with whom,' Sarah says.

That is a development that would never have been possible without the fundamental optimism of the campaigner: to believe that something ruled out by the vast majority was in fact possible.

The belief in your own ability to deliver against crazy ideas and sky-high expectations is the lifeblood of the campaigner. Martin McCourt, who until recently was the Global CEO of Dyson, told us that practicality can be a killer in business. 'Businesses that avoid the temptation to dive into execution and the fine details of product development too soon are more likely to get it right, because they focus on the full potential of what can be achieved rather than obstacles and challenges. You need to keep the idea at its highest level, being clear about what you are trying to do, what problems you are trying to solve. Pushing that idea up and widening it rather than narrowing it. In his words, 'staying as wide as possible, pushing the ideas up, is a critical part of the creative process and better ideas come to light.' Some may characterize it as gauche or naïve, but optimism is a magic ingredient for a growing company. In the face of cynicism, it is the shared belief that allows small, committed teams to deliver results that seem beyond their reach. To develop products that others deem unthinkable. And to create a culture of trust and belief which is the foundation of scalable success.

Character Building

Drive. Self-improvement. Communication. Disruption. Persuasion. Connection. Optimism. Together these seven attributes make up the characteristics of the campaigner.

'Every great change,' argues Wilfred Emmanuel-Jones, 'has come from entrepreneurial thinking. We are the people who challenge the status quo and bring about change; the pioneers that are brave enough to stand up and do it differently.'

Yet not all will be natural-born campaigners and most will need to acquire skills and habits along the way. That learning process can come out of a desire to effect a certain change within or through an organization, as in the case of Kate Robertson, who co-founded One Young World in 2010, the global annual youth forum which brings together over 1,300 young leaders from 185 countries to work collaboratively on solutions to major global problems.

'We were faced with cynicism, and faced with a faith gap where people [didn't] believe that young people had anything serious to offer,' she told us.

'I am not sure that when we had the idea for One Young World that I fully grasped I would have to campaign. In my work I am accustomed to selling, whether advertising space or public relations, but I am not accustomed to campaigning. A lot of business people are the same, but once they hit upon [campaigning] they realize it is the right way to go and something they can do.'

Indeed, with the seven character traits outlined above,

campaigning is something that anyone, from a corporate executive to an up-and-coming graduate or aspiring entrepreneur, can learn, adopt and perfect.

Portrait of a Campaigning Company

So what is a contemporary campaigning company and how can you learn from them? We spoke to Kathryn Parsons, founder of the technology education business Decoded, which wants to teach the world how to code and unlock the power of what it calls 'digital enlightenment'.

'Decoded began with a thirty-minute conversation between myself and Steve Henry, who would become my co-founder.

'The business world before we started sometimes felt quite bizarre. So much power lay in the hands of a few individuals, able to understand the language behind the screen. This had an effect on companies, on how you did business and who you hired. There was a sense of feeling dispossessed in your own workplace through this reliance on others,' she says.

'In a way, there was almost an immense fear about technology, which needed to be broken down. Even the terminology, coding, made it sound secretive and hard to understand.

'We knew this wasn't the way things had to be. Technology should be one of the most empowering and democratizing tools we have – somewhere along the line, things had gone wrong.'

The result of this was Decoded: 'That set our mission: could you take someone with no confidence or knowledge about code and teach them to the point of empowerment where they could, say, create an app from scratch? Could you demystify and decode technology to make it accessible and understandable to anyone and everyone? What's more, could you achieve all of this in a single day?'

For Parsons, it was the mission behind Decoded that drove everything forwards. 'When we started out, we didn't really have a business plan as such. Instead, we started with a mission impossible.

'When we started, there was no zeitgeist for code. It was not taught in schools. It wasn't perceived as a fundamental skill-set and literacy for a future digital economy. We realized that a huge part of our role would be campaigning to turn code from a nice-to-have to a need-to-have.'

It was soon clear this was an idea that would take off. 'From our first Code in a Day session, Decoded grew entirely from advocacy and word of mouth; ten people talked to ten people, who talked to ten people and so on,' Parsons says.

'Today we've worked with thousands of professionals teaching face-to-face, taught thousands of students online and popped up in thirty-five different cities around the world, teaching anyone from the boards of FTSE companies to mothers, career-changers, policymakers and beyond.

'What we realized was just how wide this concept of disenfranchisement was; it was there in every single geography and every single sector of society you could imagine.'

However, the success of the Code in a Day course hasn't seen Decoded rest on its laurels, running courses from cyber security to future technologies, 'letting people get hands-on in areas that they would otherwise leave to others.' Decoded has also released a free online tool, Playto.io, which allows people to learn or teach code for themselves.

Each new course is no small commitment and planned with the same care and attention as the first: 'Each of our courses take about a year to develop. We want people to come out of them thinking, that was magic, and that is why we try so hard to get them to this standard.'

For Parsons, the campaigning mentality behind Decoded has been central to its success. 'Campaigning is undoubtedly part and parcel of what we do. Going back to education, that's something that should be amazing. In recent years, technology education has been somewhat abandoned in the UK. That is changing and coding is now on the curriculum, which is a really good thing.'

As well as education, Parsons is also passionate about tackling the gender divide that exists in the technology sector: 'There is this myth we want to dispel about who should be good at this stuff, who should get this. The belief that it is something men can do better than women is total nonsense. Fifty per cent men and fifty per cent women work at Decoded and over half of the people we have taught are female. When we compare the performance, there is no difference between the two whatsoever. The only difference is that women are 30 per cent less confident to succeed at the start. This confidence issue is important. In an economy where digital confidence, skills and literacy are increasingly in demand and highly valued, women must not be excluded because of it.'

Decoded is a very clear example of a mission-driven business, something Parsons believes is becoming more prevalent. 'Our belief is crucial. How many businesses believe in what they are doing? I think that this is beginning to shift and change. That we are seeing more businesses be created with purpose at the forefront of what they do.'

Finding people to fuel that purpose within the company is part of the challenge. 'Recruitment has been the biggest learning curve for me as the business has expanded,' Parsons explains. 'It's huge. How do you find amazing technical talent? We've been lucky in the people we've found. Everyone we employ in the business is technologically skilled and a brilliant communicator. We want everyone to have high EQ [emotional], IQ [intelligence] and DQ [digital] skills.

'We try to avoid the blame game, which feels a very old-fashioned way of doing business. Rather than go, whose fault is it, we ask ourselves, why didn't that work and how can we use technology to solve the problem?'

Top Tips: Kathryn Parsons

1. **Always learning:** 'We are in the midst of a technology revolution. The world has changed beyond our imagination in the last ten years alone. As we enter an increasingly digital age, there has never been a more pressing time to be learning at all

ages and stages of our careers and education. It is something we hold dear at Decoded and internally we are constantly learning.'

2. **Impossible challenges:** 'As Walt Disney said, "It's kind of fun to do the impossible." We started with an impossible challenge and as we go forward will continue to set ourselves these goals. Ultimately, with an understanding of technology, anything is possible.'

3. **Break things:** 'As every hacker knows, making things and breaking things are one and the same. Tinker, create, test, iterate, start again and put something out into the world which you believe in.'

Building a Campaigning Company

The characteristics we have explored in this chapter begin to show how you can become a campaigner: as an entre-preneur or within your current job. They are the traits shared by many of the best and which can be studied, emulated and internalized.

But a great company cannot subsist on one, or even a handful of individuals, however talented. In the chapters ahead we will break down and examine how a business mission, and the campaigning spirit, can be franchised within a team, among your customers and the market-place at large.

We will explore how to inspire belief in a cynical marketplace, why building a company culture is essential to maintaining mission, the ways in which you communicate your purpose, the need for networks, and how to respond to setbacks. The belief on which you build your company is fundamental, but so too is the way in which you develop and share it within the organization and beyond it: that is the challenge we will now address.

Takeaways

- There are seven campaigning traits: drive, self-improvement, communication, disruption, persuasion, connection and optimism. Identify those you already possess, those that you need to work on improving, and those that are missing entirely;
- Remember that all campaigners started out small and that a large part of their success was making the most of their entrepreneurial attributes. Use their stories as inspiration to help you focus on what it is you can achieve;
- It's not just entrepreneurs who can benefit from the campaigners we've profiled. A campaigning attitude can take you to the next level of your career if you are guided by the qualities that make for business success in our fast-moving economy;
- Remember to never give up!

5

Conviction

Perception is everything. The only question is how to create
a favourable perception in the consumer's mind.
Al and Laura Ries

The principal test of any business mission is how well – to paraphrase the Prussian general Helmuth von Moltke – it survives contact with the enemy. Put another way, how can you inspire belief among consumers and build the loyalty that turns your buyers into real followers? This is what campaigners achieve: they stand out from the crowd in an age of information overload, where the pursuit of preference and the battle for attention counts for everything. It is their conviction that inspires belief in consumers and the elusive asset of trust. A business with conviction is one that can attain credibility, a hard-won prize at a time when the foundations of belief have come under question as perhaps never before.

According to the British Social Attitudes Survey, just over 50 per cent of people in the UK describe themselves as religious, down from 68 per cent in 1983. Similarly, just

18 per cent trust governments to put the national interest above their own, down from 38 per cent, and 34 per cent think banks are well run, a 56 per cent drop from three decades previously.

When the US-based Pew Research Center first asked the question, 'How much of the time do you trust the government in Washington?' in 1958, 73 per cent said they did 'most of the time'. That figure had declined to 19 per cent by the second term of the Obama presidency.

In a more untrusting society, the question has frequently been posed of how exactly people come to believe. Some posit that the new icons of faith are brands, as the ad agency Young and Rubicam claimed in 2001: 'Brands are the new religion. People turn to them for meaning.' And religion is a language that companies have long since come to embrace, with digital evangelist an increasingly common job description in the tech sector.

In this world of diminished trust and damaged institutional credibility, campaigners fill the void and offer people the belief they crave. That stands for consumers and employees alike. People want to buy from brands they find credible and wholesome; increasingly, they want to work for companies they admire as well. That is where the truly purposeful companies stand out, with a credible and meaningful reason-for-being that can inspire customers as much as it does employees.

'Even in the value end of the market, just being the right price is not enough,' TalkTalk CEO Dido Harding told us. 'It's not enough, not just for your customers, but also for your employees and for your broader stakeholders. As a brand, you need to be seen to have a slightly higher purpose than just making money. There is a much stronger debate about the ethics of business than there was a decade ago and no business can escape the need to have a position on a very large spectrum of public policy issues.'

As the popular support for traditional cornerstones such as religion and government subsides, there is a growing role for business as the sector responsible for delivering change and being worthy of trust and belief. People want to believe that they are buying the best, at the best value. That the point-of-sales promises will be fulfilled and that their judgment in choosing this brand over manifold competitors will be vindicated. Nevertheless, as the prevailing public attitude to business in the 2015 British general election campaign showed, with the association between the private sector and profiteering largely holding sway, there is still some way for business to go in showing that its conviction extends beyond making money. The idea that business can be a powerful force for good, an increasing currency among entrepreneurs and company leaders, has still to convince many within society at large.

And the challenge to business today is not so different to that faced by faith systems down the centuries. Principally in how to enlist and maintain followers: securing more converts than you lose. How to thrive in a marketplace where consumers may be investing belief as much as they do hard cash.

That creates a powerful context for campaigners, who

put the needs, desires and aspirations of their customers at the heart of their business philosophy, to prosper. They are the people who set out to build companies that are, at least in part, designed to support embattled or ignored consumers. To create a new arena of trust for people who have stopped believing.

The Power of Preference

People are not just less willing than ever before to invest their trust in institutions. They are also bombarded as never before by information, making attention a precious and hard-won asset. In a world soaked in information and where consumers are assailed on all fronts by sales messages, the power lies not in dollar-fuelled promotion, but the money-can't-buy asset of preference.

Think about the last time you really noticed an ad in the newspaper or, more importantly, when one actually prompted you to do something. Now consider reading a review in the paper or the recommendation of a friend. More often than not this will inspire action, because we are more likely to believe in the endorsement of others.

A quote that has always inspired us is from Mark McCormack, the sports agent who was the inspiration behind Jerry Maguire. 'All things being equal, people will buy from a friend. All things not being quite so equal, people will still buy from a friend,' was his dictum.

The importance of friendship in business is sorely underestimated. A customer is one thing, but an advocate is ten times more precious. Just as the Chinese proverb tells us the difference between giving a man fish and teaching him how to wield a rod, advocates give your business long-term security where a customer may be a one-hit wonder.

'Marketing by interrupting people isn't cost-effective any more . . . the future belongs to marketers who establish a foundation and process where interested people can market to each other.' That was how Seth Godin began his manifesto, *Unleashing the Ideavirus*, first published fifteen years ago but still an essential text for any campaigner.

In it he defined the essential concept of 'sneezers'. 'Sneezers are the ones who when they tell ten or twenty or 100 people – people believe them,' he wrote. A company's idea is like a virus and you need sneezers to spread that message. It's no good thinking that a team of ten, twenty or even 100, armed with more digital channels than you can shake a stick at, can get your message to where it needs to be.

People may listen to what you want to tell them. But chances are they will only really believe it when they hear someone else saying the same thing. That is the power of preference and it is at the very heart of the battle for success in today's business marketplace.

Ovo Energy: Breaking Through

The story of Stephen Fitzpatrick and Ovo Energy, the UK's fastest growing energy provider, offers a notable example of not only how to win preference in this complex and ultra-competitive market but also of a company inspired by the conviction of its campaigning founder to stand up for the consumer.

In energy start-up Ovo, Fitzpatrick's aim was to challenge the traditional providers who dominated the market. 'The focus was very much born out of a frustration,' he told us. 'Everybody else was doing it so badly, there was more of a challenge: surely it can't be this difficult to sell energy. There must be a better way to do this,' he believed.

'Rather than using all of their knowledge about consumer behaviour and the energy market to help customers use less energy and save money, the focus of the Big Six energy companies seemed to be on keeping those customers paying as much as possible, for as long as possible.'

Ovo, founded in 2009, wants 1 million customers by 2017. One of the defining moments in this journey was Fitzpatrick's appearance at a British Parliamentary Energy Select Committee hearing in November 2013, which took place at the height of a national outcry around energy prices.

'It looks to me like a lot of energy companies, a significant number of the Big Six, are charging the maximum price they feel they can get away with to the customers that they feel will not switch under any circumstance,' he told the committee. 'I've been somewhat confused by looking at the explanations for the price rises . . . because we don't see nearly the same impact, especially on wholesale commodity costs.'

In a debate that was meant to be the Big Six on trial,

Ovo dominated the headlines and, within weeks, 20,000 new customers were on its books.

When the company turned up the volume with a Valentine's Day advertising campaign ('Roses are red, Violets are blue. Dump the Big Six, Ovo loves you'), the effect was even more dramatic. Seventy-five thousand customers signed up within five weeks, necessitating 100 extra staff to cope with the demand.

Parliamentary select committees are an everyday occurrence, almost all without making a ripple on the public consciousness. This was headline news for days, and what it created was more than a story for the national press. It was a narrative that people bought into because they fundamentally understood and made common cause with a David taking aim at the Goliaths of the industry.

It showed that, even with the attention logjam that all companies face, it is possible to cut through and connect with customers in a way that changes buying decisions. Holding on to those customers is where the essential purpose and values of the business come into their own: living up to point-of-sale promises and doing right by the consumer.

What the Ovo story shows is that when the convictions of the business become the convictions of the customer, then you have created a powerful relationship that can transcend the challenges of connection and engagement that all companies now face.

Top Tips: Stephen Fitzpatrick

1. **Mean what you say:** 'It's very obvious to me that now consumers have so much more information on companies [that] it's impossible to fool them into thinking that you are a company that cares, that you are a values business,' Fitzpatrick says. 'There are just too many touch points and information points in today's world.

   'You really do have to live up to the promise . . . otherwise you end up spending a load of money on marketing and messaging that can be pulled apart in seconds.'

2. **Create the culture, don't enforce it:** 'You create parameters. Once you start to tell people exactly what you want done, the next day they will come back to you with another question . . . There is a limit to how many subjects any one person can really understand, and make decisions on. I give our people the framework within which they have the freedom to do what's right.'

3. **Do right by the customer:** 'Over time, we have developed much more of a philosophy in trying to align our interests with our customers. We spend a lot of time thinking about what is best for customers. Not just on a campaigning basis, but also on raw

commercial terms . . . if we can always make sure that what is best for customers is also good for our business, and vice-versa, then we never need to worry about regulation or about changes in the law. The business is by definition sustainable.'

Sir Terry Leahy: Enlisting Followers

The challenge of attracting and holding on to customers is one faced as much by corporate giants as it is by start-ups. In a world where most industries have to face digital challengers and a much broader range of competition, old certainties and market positions are falling away.

Tesco is one notable example of a fixture of the UK business landscape that has faced an erosion of its market foundations, under an onslaught from discount brands and faced with an investigation of how it has managed its accounts and supply chain. The question many have posed is, can a brand that in 2007 accounted for one in every seven pounds spent through UK shopping tills avert its precipitous decline? What has gone so badly wrong and what lessons might Tesco learn from its hugely successful past?

Undoubtedly, there was a time when Tesco owned the value market in British retail, and was as good as its positioning. We spoke to former CEO Sir Terry Leahy about his experiences in building the company into a global retail brand, enlisting and retaining customers in their millions and creating a culture to permeate a business with hundreds of thousands of employees.

'The core purpose we gave to Tesco was to create value for customers in order to earn their lifetime loyalty,' he says. 'Another way of looking at that is to create benefits for customers in order to earn their lifetime loyalty. The way we went about this was to understand people's lives better than anybody else and respond with innovative new products and services which made life a little bit easier. As a result we would earn the trust and loyalty of customers over the long term and that's how we would benefit.

'The strapline, "every little helps", was the expression of all these innovative responses to what we learned about customers and to what they needed in their lives.'

Tesco, he believes, stole a march on its competitors during his tenure by making it abundantly clear that they were putting customers first. 'Going back to the early nineties, I don't think Britain had a reputation for giving good service and I don't think supermarkets were seen as leaders amongst service organizations. What I did, probably, was to apply marketing theory, building the whole business back from customers.'

By listening to customers and going to great lengths to understand their habits and preferences, Tesco was able to outperform the competition, he believes. 'It's a rather simple view that people know their own lives best, a rather liberal or libertarian view. Whereas there's a whole class in society that believes that they know best, that people are either too ill-educated or too ill-informed and so "we know better".

'I believe differently. I think that if you listened to what people say they needed, they would tell you and all you had to do was respond.'

If listening and responding to customers was at the heart of Tesco's success under Sir Terry, the attitude to employees was no different. Sir Terry told us that, when marketing director of Tesco, his team interviewed the entire workforce over a two-year period, then 100,000 people.

'We got the Tesco values just by talking to the staff. It was the oral history of the company really . . . We asked two questions: "What do you think Tesco stands for and what do you think Tesco should stand for?" [The answers] basically became our values, which you could sum up as no one tries harder for customers and treat people like you would like to be treated. One being the external focus of the business and the other being the internal code of behaviour.

'It's terribly important that the staff believe in the basic proposition, the basic mission of the business, so that they contribute. You can't make them contribute, you can't buy their contribution fully. Ideally you get a voluntary contribution because they believe in it, they think it's worthwhile, important and something that they would like to contribute to.

'The basic appeal of helping customers in their busy lives is a very strong appeal and staff responded very strongly to that. Particularly if the way you ask them to contribute is by treating them with respect and dignity and trusting them and empowering them: it builds their self-esteem, so they get from their work a sense of purpose, a sense of self-esteem, a sense of satisfaction.'

While the brand has faced tough questions under Sir Terry's successors over its financial management and ability to cope with the challenge of digital and discount competitors, there is no doubting the conviction on which the brand's global success in the late 1990s and 2000s was based. That is that by following the customer, listening to their needs and understanding their preferences, success would come.

In many respects, today's Tesco story bears testament to how a brand can lose its way, so much so that one of its main competitors has appropriated its own strapline ('every Lidl helps'). The contrast between the Tesco we see now and the company that prospered in the 1990s and 2000s, shows that conviction is not something that can be taken for granted. Indeed, in a 2015 interview with *Panorama*, Sir Terry argued that the trust Tesco had once held among customers as the best value option had been 'eroded', leading many to shop around more. 'The one thing that was missing was this great strength of Tesco to take the pulse of the customer and know what they need today, and be prepared to change and innovate in order to respond to the customers' needs,' he argued.

The rapid decline of Tesco in the last few years shows that unless the offer to customers and the wider market is maintained, developed and grown, you lose the credibility that is so precious and hard won. You lose the conviction that made you a success in the first place.

Top Tips: Sir Terry Leahy

1. **Let the customer speak loudest:** '[Tesco] put the customers at the heart of the organization genuinely and gave them the most powerful voice within the organization. In older companies, you tended to see a more paternalistic, sometimes more patronizing view, where management was the loudest voice and sort of informed the business about what it thought customers needed.'

2. **Liberate your team:** 'Many people are fearful in big organizations and organizations that are state run. Many people are bureaucratic. Their day-to-day concerns are about keeping their job and protecting their boss. That's why they often never do anything; they know what's wrong and they know what should be done but they seem powerless. So, you've got to change that mindset if you want to get anything done.'

3. **Have the right reasons:** 'I think if you're going into business, and I do advise people this, make sure it's a business that you like and make sure that you've gone into it for a worthwhile reason, not just to make money, and try and remember what that worthwhile reason was as you go through all the struggles along the way.'

Translating Mission into Values

Purpose and belief are what no business can do without, but alone they take you only so far. To grow, that mission must be defined and communicated in a way that convinces the most important audiences – your customers and employees – that the company is worth being a part of.

And in today's increasingly transparent world, the actions of a company must live up to the full promise of the words. Says Sir Terry Leahy: 'There's a language you have to develop, a lexicon that people understand and then you communicate it. Most important of all, you have to live it, because people are more influenced by your behaviour when the words and actions align. Sometimes people, most of all politicians, have the right words but the wrong actions and that's where people get very cynical.'

Campaigning companies are those with a belief system hard-wired into the very heart of the business: a code for employees to adhere to, for customers to believe in and a lodestar by which to navigate the upheaval and change that growth demands.

The loss of faith in the traditional organs of power and influence does not mean that the urge to believe in something ever went away. And it is campaigners, those with a higher purpose and will to drive real change, who capture that mindshare and who provide a new arena for the most traditional and fundamental of human impulses: to congregate, collaborate and share ideas, experiences and faith.

Conquering Cynicism

The business world is no different from any other in the balance between optimists and pessimists. What campaigners represent is the extreme end of the former mentality, a boundless belief in what is possible and their ability to deliver it.

Rohan Silva, a former special adviser to Prime Minister David Cameron, who has gone on to found shared workspace Second Home, put it to us that 'one of the things that is so easy to mock about entrepreneurs and tech companies is that they really do want to have impact, they really want to change things, and often they change the world.

'I think that's a beautiful thing and it's the easiest thing to deride. I think it's something that's really precious and something we should always fight for . . . you've got a big mission and how do you keep that in your sight?'

Be in no doubt, this mindset will jar with as many people as it inspires, and it is true that business has done much in recent years that contributes to that lack of trust, with a raft of mis-selling scandals to name just one example. However, beyond a natural level of caution and distrust, and particularly in the UK, many are hard-wired to a cynical mentality that arguably limits ideas and ambition. They are the people who US President Teddy Roosevelt famously skewered as, 'cold and timid souls who neither know victory nor defeat'.

Over a hundred years ago, Roosevelt summed up what it still means to be a campaigner: 'It is not the critic who counts; not the man who points out how the strong man stumbles, or where the doer of deeds could have done them better,' he said.

'The credit belongs to the man who is actually in the arena, whose face is marred by dust and sweat and blood; who strives valiantly; who errs, who comes short again and again . . . but who does actually strive to do the deeds; who knows great enthusiasms, the great devotions; who spends himself in a worthy cause.'

If you are building a business, the Roosevelt 'critics' will surround you at every turn and a small, dangerous word will become your companion in the first flush of trading. No. That sole syllable is the campaigner's constant foe in the early days as you try to convince your first employees, suppliers and clients.

The first instinct of every established entity will be to say no. They don't need it, they've heard it all before, they're already quite well set, it is too risky. The tales of greatness born from rejection are legion. 'Guitar groups are on their way out,' was the oft-quoted response from industry mogul Dick Rowe when approached by Brian Epstein in 1962 about a young band called the Beatles. George Orwell faced the same when he first pitched *Animal Farm* to publishers. 'It is impossible to sell animal stories in the USA,' was one notable reply.

Overwhelming indifference will be the default response of many. And that is where the zeal, belief and sheer persistence of the campaigner come to the fore. Against the persistent undercurrent of pessimism, the campaigner's greatest friend is another small word. Yes.

Try saying it when you want to say no, when you find yourself opening your mouth to say maybe. Try saying yes to that meeting that looks like a dead end, or that party that just seems like too much trouble after a long week.

Many of the best things we have achieved in the last five years happened because we said yes to opportunities that looked far from gift-wrapped on first appearance. We have met people, struck up relationships and forged partnerships that could never have come about without the essential optimism that 'yes' demands of you.

For campaigners the power of yes is absolute and fundamental. It defines your willingness to engage and to innovate. To adopt and develop niches which have been written off by others as too difficult, time-consuming or outlandish to be worth considering.

In 2010, just months after starting up, we decided we would create an event the UK lacked – a national festival for entrepreneurs. We called it MADE, and set course for Michael's home city of Sheffield. The received wisdom was that we were mad: what right did an unknown start-up have to speak for the country's entrepreneurs; and what insanity led them to think it could work in a post-industrial city in the north of England?

One very senior business journalist told us that he had never heard a worse idea. Two years later, MADE had become a 3,000-person event, the established expo for entrepreneurship, and a campaign for Britain's entrepreneurs to be proud of.

The lesson is this. By all means, take all the advice you can get, hear the counsel of those who have been before you and who have experienced the slings and arrows of a business journey. But when you have a fundamental belief in what you are seeking to do, don't let people who purport to know better convince you otherwise, and resist the siren to lower expectations.

Sometimes the numbers will not add up, the proposition cannot be viewed by many as sound and the chances of success seem slim. It is often at such moments that you are on the verge of something brilliant, but it takes every ounce of conviction, determination and sheer bloody-mindedness not just to deliver, but to continue seeking the opportunity in the first place. Beware letting the cynics erode your conviction and sense of purpose.

Takeaways

- Consumers are becoming increasingly cynical. Belief is on the wane, from government to established religion and big institutions. Campaigning companies can fill this void and show consumers that they can believe in something better;
- If campaigners can live up to the expectations of their customers by living the values their missions preach, then they are able to create a band of followers – or advocates – whose

recommendations continue to spread the
word;

- Followers must be looked after for the long term.
Campaigners are able to place themselves in the
shoes of their customers and look after their
needs as they would their own;
- A campaigner is relentlessly focused on the trust
of their consumers, and most importantly, will
practise what they preach.

6

Culture

Tribes form horizontally. Change happens from person to person, rarely from the top down.

Seth Godin

Entrepreneurship is often wrongly characterized as a lone-wolf activity, but as a founder you quite quickly reach the limits of what you can achieve alone. And if you want to go from being a lone voice to a true campaigning machine, you need people who will buy into your mission and develop, build and sustain it. In the next two chapters, we will look at how you can achieve this. First, how you can build a team, by creating a culture that is as strong and enduring as the mission you began with. Then, how you extend that beyond your company, by making connections with the right people who can help you grow and develop your business.

Culture is about style of working and a company's fundamental purpose, but in a campaigning environment it is also about progress and achievement. A campaigning culture is above all one that liberates talent, an ambitious ambience where high-performance is incubated and rewarded. At the same time it is rooted in a fundamental set of beliefs about an organization's ability to change things and deliver on its mission. Those are the values which, when properly expressed, act as a shared code of conduct and provide common terms of engagement with colleagues and the outside world.

The culture and values of the business act as your anchor and reference point, focusing minds on the essential mission and purpose, a check on decision-making and priorities. Your culture should be informed by the mission you have set and communicated via your story.

But a culture is not simply or quickly forged. Most business owners would tell you that recruitment is one of the biggest challenges they face. In campaigning companies this is especially true because you are trying to build a very definitive house style, in which everyone captures the same ethos. It's not just the talent to get the job done that you're recruiting but the ambition and desire to be part of something bigger and better.

When you start a company your purpose and form is at its purest: a streamlined philosophy and methodology for delivering success. You are small, perfectly formed and focused in everything you do.

A bigger team means people who need to be convinced of the integrity of your purpose as much as the founders. It also means the gradual increase of structures and processes that can be held off no longer as your numbers grow.

To avoid the fatal dilution of purpose that made you strong in the first place, you need the mission behind a company to become a culture that can be franchised through a team of people, a core of advocates and ultimately a base of customers.

Culture matters because in the life of a business there quickly comes a point where the founding team can no longer see or influence all, or indeed most, of what goes on in the business they created. An ethos created by an individual or small band of people can only scale as a culture that can be shared, nurtured and grown by a team of many.

As the marketeer Seth Godin has written: 'Tribes form horizontally. Change happens from person to person, rarely from the top down. Organizations establish a culture, the way we do things around here, as much from the craftsmen on the shop floor as from what the CEO does in her office.'

The need for an authentic and robust culture is what makes building a team an arduous but also particularly rewarding process for many entrepreneurs. You are looking not just for people with the talent to deliver results but who can both fit in with and amplify the ethos of the business. Founders who have built businesses with social purpose at their heart want to recruit a team as committed and enthusiastic as they are. In the view of Ella's Kitchen's Paul Lindley: 'You need an exceptional, fantastic team that can take the seed of your crazy idea and actually deliver it, add to it, embellish it and be passionate about it.'

It is the culture, expressed through values that steer everything from recruitment to everyday operations, that distinguishes campaigning companies. And it is through its culture, which should be a live and constantly adapting ethos, that the idea behind a business starts to take hold and mature into a sustainable reality.

What follows are the stories of three companies where culture – its creation, development and redevelopment – has played a notable role, from the start-up phase to high growth and the public market. Firstly Unruly, which prides itself on maintaining its start-up ethos as it grows; secondly dunnhumby, where the founders created a distinctive culture based around people to grow the business abroad; and thirdly TalkTalk, where chief executive Dido Harding had to overhaul the company culture as part of her turnaround drive. The stories show how motivated leaders have been able to get the best out of their teams through the environment they have created. They demonstrate that culture is an essential part of successful businesses at all stages of development.

Start-up Culture: Unruly

Campaigning companies are by their nature fast-paced, no more so than those in the technology sector. A case in point is video ad tech company Unruly, one of the UK's fastest-growing tech firms and the world's leading social video platform, specializing in making branded video content go viral.

As one of the pioneers of online content sharing, it has seen the market for social video sky-rocket: co-founder Sarah Wood, a Cambridge academic turned entrepreneur, told us that when the company started, Dove had set the bar with 60,000 shares for its Real Beauty campaign. Now, as Unruly's Viral Video Chart of most-shared ads demonstrates, over a million shares in a week is not unusual.

At the crest of the online sharing wave, Unruly has had to constantly adapt to stay ahead of the market. That has meant new products that at first pass seemed impossible, notably a proprietary algorithm that allows the company to predict the viral success of a brand video.

The constant need to innovate is something that has been hard-wired into the culture and values of Unruly, codified as embracing change, sharing the love and delivering wow.

'Those values are really seminal and the embrace change is probably the most important of the three,' Wood says, 'because we're constantly innovating and bringing in new ideas. So we hire for it, we hire for those values.'

In her view, 'We will never stop being a start-up because for me that is about innovation, it's about being scrappy, about being lean, it's about using imagination.

'In today's business environment, where there are seismic changes happening all across the world, no one is exempt from the changes that are going on. Even the largest companies need to adopt an agile start-up mentality to help them succeed in a fast-moving market.'

In that context, putting an ambitious but manageable culture of change at the heart of how the company operates has been crucial to its success. 'Clear communication is the biggest challenge as you grow quickly. When it's just three of us we can just innovate just like that, but when you've got 200 people and you're trying to innovate rapidly, it can be challenging. At Unruly we practise what we call extreme communications: we talk to each other all the time. It's about making sure there are no knowledge gaps, making sure knowledge is spread as wide as possible across the business. This is good for both business continuity, but also personal development, because it means there is a constant impetus for people to share their ideas and share their knowledge with each other.'

The role of the company founders can evolve into one where they are custodians of the culture, Wood says. 'A lot of people look at the founders for guidance, so having the values there is incredibly helpful when things change. People come to me and say things are changing and I say yes, it's because we embrace change! It's nothing to be afraid of, cultures will evolve, and products will evolve.'

In creating a set of values and a conscious culture around change, Unruly has been able to stay ahead of the competition and build an ever-growing team – now over 200 across fifteen offices, gaining recognition as one of the 'Future 50' companies driving the UK's digital economy – that shares and amplifies the vision of its three founders and is leading the company on to ever greater success.

Top Tips: Sarah Wood

1. **Involve the team:** In a fast-growing and fast-moving environment, there is a need to keep your team engaged and involved in decision-making. 'OneRuly' town hall meetings of the entire team are used to set and share strategic priorities and involve the whole company in decision-making. 'Each year we will tend to have at least one all-company session where everyone has an opportunity to publicly share and stand up for their ideas.'

2. **Build squads:** 'Whenever we've got a big project we have a squad. We create a squad especially for that project and they're cross-functional. The squads allow people to take on projects and lead projects even if they're not leading in specific teams . . . It's really helpful for Unruly to have those squads, because we can surface leaders, we can surface rising stars and give them development opportunities without it being too permanent. You can give more junior people a chance to shine and to prove themselves.'

3. **Incentivize culture:** 'On an individual level we have a match-giving programme. So every Unruly [team member] has £500 available each year and if they raise up to £500 for their good cause we will match that . . . Where it's nicest of all is when the

> teams come together, so we have [had] ten people
> doing a run in the London parks . . . they'll often
> have shared causes that we can get behind and
> really enjoy.'

Growth Culture: dunnhumby

For a growing business, culture is a precious and fragile asset. It is what can enable sustainable growth yet it is also put at risk every step further the company takes from base camp.

That is especially true when a business is expanding into global markets. The challenge of packaging and exporting the ethos that has made the domestic operation successful is critical. This was the challenge faced by Edwina Dunn and Clive Humby, the husband and wife duo who founded big data insight and targeting company dunnhumby, the force behind Clubcard, the loyalty innovation widely credited with helping to establish Tesco as a global retail force in the 1990s and 2000s.

What Clubcard and its offshoots enabled for retailers was a whole new form of engagement with customers: not just rewarding them for their purchases, but collecting and aggregating shopping till data to create an unprecedented picture of who these customers were, how they shopped and what motivated their purchases.

'Retailers had their eyes opened to the reality that there is no such thing as an average customer,' Clive recalls. 'I think one of the great fallacies of the industry was that the average customer spends £30 a week and fits into this neat box. The insight was that this was actually not true; customers like luxury products and value ingredients in the same shopping trip – scrimp and splurge. It is all about understanding this complex mix and meeting both these needs and multiple price points.'

A better understanding of the buyer realities, Edwina says, allowed retailers to build more meaningful relationships with their customers. 'Driving action from data means you have to give customers value for the exchange – something they want, like relevant information, better service and engaging offers. And you have to keep learning and adding value. It's relentless and changing.'

Launched from the kitchen table of its founding couple in 1989, dunnhumby focused unstintingly on putting the customer first. 'We've always seen ourselves as a customer champion,' says Edwina, '[being] the voice of the customer at the board level. Most boards talk about having a customer champion, but practically none of them do. It's one of those things where they don't know how to turn it into a job description or where it fits in the marketing, commercial and IT mix, and so it doesn't happen.'

As well as seeking to create a new category within marketing, Dunn and Humby were dealing with a rapidly evolving technology landscape. 'Insight once a quarter became daily insight,' Dunn says. 'Now it's more like hour-by-hour. And that demands huge change and transformation within the business and across its operating model.'

Riding the wave of that change, dunnhumby grew into a global force in the 1990s and 2000s, with over 1,500 people working in twenty-five countries when the founders stepped away in 2011. The model they developed to achieve this was the Power of Two, the pairing up of two people with complementary skills to lead the launch of a regional office in each new market. Dunnhumby's operations in the US, France, India and markets around the world came not off the back of invading armies, but teams, like the founders, that came in pairs.

'What I found is that as soon as you put a team together, people hid behind others and people who were often extremely good didn't speak out,' Dunn told us. 'The idea was if you had two people there was nowhere for anybody to hide. It both scared and energized them and it pushed them out of their comfort zones. But I think out of absolute urgency and often a degree of fear, individuals end up doing some amazing things. It was definitely a model when people talked about it afterwards and said, "It was the scariest thing I ever did but it was the thing that changed me the most." And it's addictive.'

The fundamental insight, Humby reflects, was in prioritizing complementary strengths and not focusing on individual weaknesses. 'You didn't need anyone to be good at everything, because actually those people are like hen's teeth,' he says. 'We went from one country with Tesco, to two with Kroger and then to thirty countries in the space of a couple of years [and that] was the only way we could do it.'

Top Tips: Edwina Dunn and Clive Humby

1. **Pair opposites:** The success of the dunnhumby Power of Two method was not based around people who necessarily got on well. 'It had to be people who didn't necessarily like each other the most, they often irritated the hell out of each other because they were opposites,' Dunn says.

2. **Hire young:** 'Young, clever people . . . are actually some of the best people to work with because they don't have preconceived ideas and they haven't learned behaviours around policy and why you can't do something,' Dunn says. 'Take bright young people who are naturally collaborative and they break all the rules and they build something better, stronger, newer, because they don't know anything else.'

3. **Find a way:** Once Dunn and Humby knew they had to expand overseas, they faced a supply problem of talent: people with the requisite skills. 'We suddenly had to go global and we didn't have enough people who understood what we did. So we had to find the leanest model, to find a way to make them go further.' That realization was what brought about the Power of Two and the model that started the company's massive growth phase into the multi-billion pound entity it is today.

Corporate Culture: TalkTalk

When Dido Harding was recruited to lead TalkTalk in 2010, the telecoms provider and Carphone Warehouse offshoot was being prepared for a stock market flotation. Yet TalkTalk's growth, though rapid, was uneven and in many ways destabilizing, leading to a welter of customer complaints and supply issues. 'It was a very chaotic, very fast-growing entrepreneurial business, that has been very much focused on being the right price and trying to democratize the technology,' Harding says. 'But in the process, systems and processes were causing problems for customers and our reputation was bad, no doubt about it.'

How, then, was she able to turn around a company with rock-bottom customer satisfaction ratings and falling subscriptions, into the provider that is now seeing steady growth and which last year became the UK's fastest-growing pay-TV provider?

With customers, 'We had to do some things which other people weren't doing, to demonstrate that we really meant it about being more customer-driven,' Harding told us.

The answer was HomeSafe, a parental control and cyber security platform, which was offered to customers for free. 'We helped our competitors work out how to do it too and set up an industry joint venture to promote Internet safety. We did that consciously because we knew that we couldn't just fix our customer issues and that wouldn't be enough.'

Just as customer loyalty had to be won over, internal

culture was also in a state of disrepair when Harding took the job. 'When I arrived . . . nobody said they worked for TalkTalk, they all said they were "ex-Carphone" or "ex-Onetel": everybody was "ex-something".

'We had to start from scratch, bottom up and top down, deciding what do we want to stand for. I went round and spoke to people face-to-face in groups of about a hundred, one after another, and encouraged them to give me feedback,' Harding recalls. 'The front line of an organization, public or private, always knows what's wrong. They might not know how to solve it, but they will always tell you the problems if you're brave enough to hear it. Out of that immersive research came the "Brighter basics", five values ranging from "it's not just about the money" to "we zig when the world zags".'

Keeping a close ear to the ground with employees and customers alike, 'listening to the river – putting yourself in the miseries and the pain', as Harding puts it, remains essential for ensuring that the company culture is maintained and strengthened. 'I'm quite a big believer in the emotional engagement of your customers with the brand. I'm a retailer at heart and another thing that retailers can do is start walking into a shop every day and start talking to customers.

'I haven't got any shops to walk into, but I can talk to customers by email; I can go into the call centre and listen to the calls and I can talk to the agents, and if I speak to them, then I can talk to the customers in the call centres as well, which is always really good fun.'

Above all, Harding says, a renewed sense of purpose has helped lift the culture at the formerly beleaguered outfit. 'We care deeply about digital inclusion; we don't want to see a society where you have a group of people left behind. Our customers are often the less wealthy in society and less digitally confident, which we can help with.

'We care about making the Internet a safer place: we can't make it completely safe, but we can make it a safer place. We've found that campaigning – internally and externally – actually makes TalkTalk just a better place to work for everybody and it makes us, our employees and our customers, proud.'

Top Tips: Dido Harding

1. **Talk to customers:** 'I reply to every customer complaint, every email I get every day. I spend at least an hour a day reading what customers are saying. My top team all get copied in on all the responses, so we really try to hear the stuff that's not good, and to feel it, because I think you have to feel these things as well as analytically measure them.'

2. **Practise what you preach:** 'When I arrived at TalkTalk almost none of our engineers had TalkTalk products at home,' Harding says. She worked to encourage all employees to start using TalkTalk, 'to eat their own cooking and to have that pride in it'.

3. **Invest in management:** Internal communication is vital to build a company culture, but it cannot begin and end with the senior leadership, Harding says. 'I had to work really hard with my management team [on internal communication] when I joined, because it wasn't something they thought was their job. We had to work really, really hard with people to make them understand how important communication is.'

The Business Family

There is an old adage: 'families that eat together stay together', and the world of work could well take a few lessons from the home environment.

Family is one word that may explain why some businesses are called 'special'. It is not a biological definition, more a state of mind.

Not every business has it, but for those that do, it is a delicate but potent part of what makes them strong. It refers to the closeness, affection and attitude that bind people together and make them win. It is how you can tell if the culture is working or not.

It is an ideal. It seems to us that many entrepreneurs are running companies that are special because they act more like committed parents than plutocrats.

'Our people are just like family.' It can sometimes sound like a terrible cliché, but people say it for a reason. The word family is an emotive and powerful one. Employees who feel part of a working family have a sense of belonging; customers sense the magic; and the business glows if its brand halo is brightened by the sense of family.

There are very practical reasons why people respond so powerfully to the working family ideal. The average person spends about 48 to 50 'conscious' hours in a week with working colleagues as compared to only 34 'conscious' hours with family members. If you are going to spend so much of your life at work then it is natural that you want to have a sense of belonging.

Creating a sense of belonging means you are more likely to give more, work harder, be more committed. Many are wary of firms that celebrate the family ideal. It implies hierarchy, sentimentalism and false ideals. Yet the rewards far outstrip the risks. It is the very absence of a sense of family that makes many bureaucracies and large corporations struggle to find a common identity and sense of purpose.

No amount of branding gloss can fabricate the authenticity of family. So if you've got it, flaunt it. The most dangerous moment for any family brand is when it reaches a size where it risks losing the magic. Then the family must be turned into a tribe.

The tribal instinct is vital because it is based on bonds of trust, forged in the heart of challenging circumstances, long hours and victory against the odds. What may start as a group of individuals can become a team where people instinctively trust in their abilities to deliver and to support one another.

Basic human instinct is that when you become part of a tribe, leaving is a wrench. And while volatility and departure are an inevitable part of the business world, binding people to a cause which they can believe in is the most powerful way of both attracting and retaining the talent you need to grow.

So, beware the moment when the people around you start to describe your team as 'human capital', or when the tragedy of redundancy becomes 'natural wastage'. Modern management speak is the antithesis of the business cultures we are referring to.

In turn, it is a myth to believe that family can only apply to businesses of a certain size. We think it is a concept at the heart of many entrepreneurial businesses, both large and small.

When you create a business you create a family, which is exactly what we have experienced with Seven Hills. The business has its proverbial brothers and sisters, newborns and moody teenagers. Dysfunctional yet devoted, bonkers yet brilliant, it has always been the particular mix of family that makes the firm special.

Our politicians certainly are wise to the potent symbolism of the family. When they champion 'hard working families' it is as much about an ideal as it is actual people. But politicians struggle with evoking the authenticity of family. All too often the magic seems to disappear into fabricated and manufactured mantras. It is a concept that somehow seems to diminish when a political stranger tries to apply it to you.

In the home and certain workplaces it is different. Why? Because it is authentic and true.

Silicon Valley: Home of the Brave

The campaigning culture within a company can be supported and amplified by the wider environment in which it operates. We have reason to regularly visit Silicon Valley, and have witnessed a place that acts as a magnet for those with towering ambitions and a fearless optimism about what they can achieve.

Over a quarter of a million Brits are estimated to live in the Bay Area and they are helping to build nothing less than a new world capital for the confident.

Take Michael Birch, the understated founder of Bebo, who exited for a cool $850 million and described the culture to us like this: 'There is a fearless belief that you can achieve anything here.'

Huddle's Andy McLoughlin came to the Valley on the mantra of 'Go Big or Go Home' and he told us that, 'Everyone here is focused on making a world-beating company. We came out here in 2007 and you could immediately feel the palpable energy.'

Simon Segars, the chief executive of ARM Holdings, arguably Britain's most successful technology firm, agrees. 'The spirit of entrepreneurialism here is unique, really quite special,' he said. 'If you look at our HQ it is [like] the United Nations. People from all over the world flock here.'

That accumulation of the world's talent builds a velocity of creativity in the Valley. In the reception of one corporation we visited, on display is the Einstein quote: 'Creativity is contagious. Pass it on.'

The culture of the San Francisco Bay Area is one that is utterly future focused and where ambition is off the scale. Much of that stems from the sheer size of the region, which is hard to take in as a first-time visitor. The Valley is a river of capital flowing 1,800 square miles with over twenty of the Fortune 500 based there. US venture firms invested $13 billion in 1,114 start-ups in the second quarter of 2014, with a significant proportion of that money going to Valley companies.

The fearless, limitless culture this creates is the ideal environment for campaigners and fosters a spirit of relentless ambition and optimism. 'People in their twenties have no clue about what can't be done, they just set about solving the problem,' says Jon Reynolds, founder of language technology company SwiftKey, which powers smartphone keyboards and has offices in both London and San Francisco.

If the ambient culture of the Valley plays a significant role in the success of its resident companies, so too does the sheer profusion of entrepreneurs and start-ups; the cluster effect of so many companies congregating and the resulting collision of talent and ideas. It is the world's leading example of the benefits a strong external environment can bring to a business, something that must be sought and cultivated as assiduously as internal culture.

Indeed, the strength of the Valley's entrepreneurial culture has led some to call for the UK to develop its own equivalent. Peter Jones CBE, the founding *Dragons' Den* panellist, has long contended that the UK needs its own 'British Dream', an equivalent of the iconic American mantra.

'Children need to be introduced to [commercial] ideas early,' he has written. 'Our counterparts in the US are masters of this – their kids are brought up thinking they can be whatever they want to be. Their "American Dream" pushes millions to try for the unrealistic and unlikely – and consequently they gave birth to the Mark Zuckerbergs and Steve Jobs of this world. We need our children to have this attitude – and to develop their very own British Dream,' he says.

That Silicon Valley, underpinned by the fundamental ideal of the American Dream, continues to hold a magnetic power within the business world, is ample testament to the power of culture and environment in today's commercial landscape.

Building Your Culture

At its simplest, a strong campaigning culture is about the identification and inspiration of great people. It is the team on which a company will ultimately stand and fall, and the leadership of a business must work hard to nurture a shared sense of ownership, mission and accomplishment.

We believe that four essential traits are at the heart of great campaigning teams:

i) **Grip:** Getting hold of an issue or project and quickly assessing how progress can most quickly and effectively be made. In the foothills of daunting assignments, it is all too easy for teams to talk themselves into paralysis. The best people identify the immediate actions and solutions, which create the internal momentum to solve the greater problems at hand.

ii) **Bite:** This is tenacity, the refusal to give in. Sometimes you will have to accept no for an answer, but what is never acceptable is neglecting to pose the question in the first place. Piling up rejections is what gets to the most precious and hard-won successes and that is what we like to see from the team.

iii) **Pounce:** Jumping on opportunities the moment they emerge, with speed of response and delivery the key. Chance encounters and sales openings are all around you, but it often means extra work and diverting off-plan to take advantage. You want a team that is flexible, imaginative and willing to respond to opportunities as they arise.

iv) **Surge:** When the team comes together as one, pooling people against a blockage or particular concern. Some of our best successes come when we focus the collective knowledge and thinking of the company on a difficult question to get over the hurdles that will inevitably emerge.

A team with these attributes is one with a driving sense of purpose, imbued with activism, enterprise and optimism. These are the ingredients we see in teams that believe they can achieve almost anything.

Above all these are the assets of an active rather than passive business mentality, the absolute mark of the campaigning company. In many workplaces the mindset can prevail that hard work of itself is virtuous, that turning up to work is the same as working, that time at the desk somehow equates to endeavour.

A campaigning founder or CEO sets an energetic agenda for the team to follow and shapes a culture around change: momentum and movement in the place of process, driving forward where others hold back to take stock.

The campaign is a relentless process; it requires a team of people with the constitution to thrive in a high-intensity environment where what is great today will only be good tomorrow, and the urgent need to be ahead trumps all.

Our message to the team is always this: never forget what you can do. Only you really know if you're living up to your potential; only you know if you are putting your heart and soul into delivering, squeezing out every opportunity. And it matters, because individual effort and aptitude is what adds up to deliver the power of the team.

Takeaways

- Culture is the critical link between an entrepreneur's founding vision and its manifestation as a real business. It is a company's values made real;
- Culture is about style of working and a company's fundamental purpose, but in a campaigning environment it is also about progress and achievement;
- The role of the company founders can evolve into one where they are custodians of the culture, instilling the right values and behaviours into an ever-growing team;
- The culture of Silicon Valley is one that is future focused and where ambition is measured by the bucket-load. The fearless, limitless culture this creates is the ideal environment for campaigners and fosters a spirit of relentless ambition and optimism. Try to cultivate that spirit of bravery and creativity within your own campaigning business;
- There are four essential traits at the core of any campaigning team. We call these grip, bite, pounce and surge.

7

Collaboration

All things being equal, people will buy from a friend. All things not being quite so equal, people will still buy from a friend.
Mark McCormack

Planting your flag as a plucky start-up is one thing, but beginning to punch through to the wider market, to gain traction and compete with entities that dwarf you, is a whole other level of challenge. This is where the power of mission and the arts of campaigning come to the fore, none more so than networking and collaboration.

One thing we have learned in five years of running our own business is that you can achieve a great deal in a short time, but only if the right people are on your side. You need the right partners and collaborators: employees and clients for sure, but also a network of broader contacts and friends who identify with what you are trying to achieve and work with you in any number of ways to support those aims.

When we went into business together it was with almost forty working years' combined experience and contacts in our industry. The amazing thing is quite how quickly you reach the end of what you can achieve via people you already know. A former boss made the point to us not long after we had started: your existing network will run dry within months, half a year if you are lucky. The viability of your business rests on your ability to build new relationships, to grow your black book and accumulate contacts on an almost competitive basis.

By making friends, entrepreneurs drive their businesses forward. And they do it well because the ability to persuade is hard-wired into the modus operandi of the successful founder. Based on little more than the force of belief and ideas, you have to convince all number of different people, from your first hire to your first client, that they should give you a go. And once you have become interesting, the campaign soon turns into a club that people want to join.

It is at the tipping point between communication and advocacy that you start to achieve real cut-through and influence. Campaigns sell on belief and the army that they build is one that wants to make others believe. That is how you go from a great idea to making a real impact: not just people or promotions that you pay for, but individuals who believe in you and want to tell the world just what a great thing they've discovered.

With the right supporters you quickly become remarkable; a conversation point. Your network is what makes you powerful, whether you are starting or growing a business or making your way up the career ladder. You become influential and important, as an organization or individual, by dint of the networks you create. In the five years running our own business we have probably met and networked with more people than we had during our entire previous careers.

For some, networking is something to be approached with caution, the subject of apprehension and even dislike. But the important point is that the opportunity is a universal one. Never let a friend, business partner or employee tell you that it is hard to meet people, unless they are working off a remote Pacific island. The plethora of free events on offer in most major cities makes it easy to find potential contacts, clients and employees if you show enough willingness and enthusiasm for the cause.

That is to say nothing of the digital tools at your disposal, and in business there is very little room left for those who disdain platforms like Twitter. In our interconnected world, rich in conversation and dialogue, you have to look as professional and open online as you do in person.

Social media is hardly the sum of contemporary business but it is a unique conversation starter. A chance approach or interaction could be what leads to a meeting that lands a new assignment, uncovers a fresh opportunity or a potential recruit. Online and on the ground, you have to be out there to thrive in a competitive, connected business landscape. Put yourself at the heart of the conversation or watch others reap the benefit of collaboration at your expense.

Throw That Party

For the campaigner, collaboration comes in many forms. A good part of it is a diligent, boots on the ground approach to networking and developing new contacts. Attending the right events, hunting down speaker and media opportunities, getting the right invitations to create a platform for yourself and your brand. These are the fundamentals of good business and managing your own reputation, be it on behalf of a business you own or one you work for.

As well as taking advantage of what is out there and making yourself a part of a scene that already exists, you need to seize people's attention and rally people to your cause. To make a splash on your own terms and where people can see your personal brand in action.

Unruly founder Sarah Wood told us the story of how, at a formative stage, her company used the launch of the government's Tech City programme to borrow some limelight and attention.

'Probably the best hour I ever spent at Unruly was organizing a flash mob outside the launch of Tech City, when David Cameron announced it in November 2010. It was happening at the building we were in at the time.

'There were twenty of us at that point: we had cushions made with the Unruly logo and Twitter, Facebook and YouTube links on them and we stood outside in a row holding them in front of our faces. When all the VIPs came out and I was standing by the door handing out business cards, half the people were asking if Unruly were sponsoring the event and the other half if we were picketing it. That was the great and good of the dotcom era; we were on ITN and the background of lots of other news broadcasts.

'That was a great example of growth hacking and doing something that was agile, imaginative and took very little cash, just a bit of courage.'

In building our own business we have frequently hosted events ranging from parties to debates and major conferences that primarily serve as an opportunity to bring interesting people together under our metaphorical (sometimes actual) roof. That means investing cash and time to create something that people want to attend and which wows them from start to finish.

In our very early days we put approximately 15 per cent of the company's cash behind a launch event to introduce ourselves to the market in style.

We gathered 250 of the most influential people in London together and by so doing let a room full of potential clients know that we had the ambition to think big from day one. The party delivered what we needed: enquiries and leads that justified the significant cash outlay.

If you want to be a market leader then you have to act like one, even when your ambitions may be some way ahead of the reality. Sometimes you just have to take the risk. And throw the party.

The Power of Partnership

The importance of collaboration may primarily be with external friends and partners, but do not underestimate the importance of partnership at the heart of your own organization. Everyone loves a good double act and that lesson applies as much in business as it does in comedy.

On one level it provides you with a formidable asset when making deals: it can be a phenomenal and flamboyant part of the showmanship of business, doubling your chances of the sale. If someone doesn't like you then the arrival of the partner can often give you a second bite at the cherry, something we have had first-hand experience of.

It's also an important asset for the ballast and substance of a business. If you get it right then the two personalities can make a perfect whole. It can balance you, enhance decision-making, and boost your stamina.

In our industry it also gives you a head start. Twice the experience, twice the contacts, twice the ideas. But perhaps most importantly, twice the courage.

When we established our business we were inspired in the early days by the story of the advertising agency Saatchi & Saatchi – a company shaped by two restless thinkers who delivered campaigns that captured mindshare and made a difference. For many years the brand Saatchi & Saatchi helped define British creativity and it was built on the pioneering power of partnership. 'Maurice could never have created the ads without Charles,' says one industry figure quoted by the *Daily Beast*, 'but Charles could never have created the agency without Maurice.'

Some of the most successful businesses in the world, the titanic brands of our age, have been built through the strength of partnership. Take Mr Rolls and Mr Royce, Mr Marks and Mr Spencer, Mr Goldman and Mr Sachs, or Mr Hewlett and Mr Packard, to name but a very few.

What's more, brands like Apple and Microsoft were built on partnership. Bill Gates may be the one we remember from Microsoft but his co-founder Paul Allen lives with an estimated fortune of $15 billion, as one of the richest men in America today.

And it doesn't stop there. Even Gates and Steve Jobs, renowned for one of the most titanic commercial struggles of our age, worked as collaborators at various points, including in 1997, the year Jobs returned to Apple as CEO, when Microsoft invested $150 million into the then-struggling business.

Of course partnerships can bring as much strife as they do success and what starts as the ultimate pairing can easily collapse into acrimony. *Bridge Over Troubled Water* sunk the friendship of Simon and Garfunkel. The tempestuous relationship between Jack Dorsey and Ev Williams could have cost the world Twitter, while German brothers Adolf and Rudolf Dassler famously fell into irreconcilable conflict over their co-owned shoe business in post-war Germany. The result was two companies which still have competing factories in the Dassler brothers' home town of Herzogenaurach: Adidas and Puma.

There is an art to it and a business partnership is something that must be tended as assiduously and caringly as any long-term relationship. But the point to remember is that two minds can be better than one and whether you are building a business or seeking to change the organization in which you work, a co-conspirator can play a huge part in helping you along the way. A campaigner who embraces the power of partnership in their business stands perhaps a better chance of fulfilling their mission than one who seeks to carve out a path alone. Indeed, we may well be entering the era of the co-founder, and our observation is that it is increasingly common to see new businesses being launched not by founding individuals, but by founding teams.

The Dirty (Half) Dozen: Creating StartUp Britain

Among entrepreneurs there is a particularly strong urge to partner and collaborate. When a group of people with the archetypal entrepreneur traits of big ideas and a refusal to take no for an answer collide, the results can be something to behold. In our own experience, the creation of the government-backed enterprise campaign StartUp Britain showed exactly what a small but committed team of collaborators can achieve: a successful national campaign, by entrepreneurs for entrepreneurs.

The campaign was born in the Cavendish Square offices

of Lord Young of Graffham, career entrepreneur and enterprise adviser to two Prime Ministers, the cabinet minister of whom Margaret Thatcher said: 'Others bring me problems, David brings me solutions.'

It was early 2011, the economy was in positive growth but only just, the number of new business registrations was down by 20,000 year-on-year and Britain was becoming embroiled in the Europe-wide row about how to rescue the continent's most stricken economies.

The meeting, between Lord Young, Michael and the other StartUp Britain co-founders (Oli Barrett, Duncan Cheatle, Rajeeb Dey, Emma Jones, Lara Morgan, Jamie Murray Wells and Richard O'Connor, later joined by Luke Johnson as chairman), was a speculative one, but out of the broad idea to help the nation's enterprise culture, the basis of a campaign soon started to emerge. A second meeting followed, then a third with the Prime Minister's then head of strategy, the uncompromising Steve Hilton.

Next we found ourselves on a train to the East Midlands, pitching the campaign first to the Prime Minister and then a full meeting of Cabinet. And within weeks we were launching the campaign at Microsoft, with the PM, Chancellor and a room packed with British business luminaries and up-and-coming talents.

In the years since, StartUp Britain has been at the heart of the boom in the UK's start-up culture. Over 580,000 new businesses were registered in 2014, while self-employment has risen to a forty-year high according to the Office for National Statistics. According to Nectar

Business, over half of 16–30-year-olds in the UK believe they will start their own business in the next five years, and 81 per cent would like to. In the view of Lord Young, 'the impact [of StartUp Britain] was tremendous . . . it set the scene nationally.' It is, he says, 'from that time that the number of start-ups went up and up.'

From a campaigning perspective, StartUp Britain offers an object lesson in the importance and effectiveness of collaboration. This was a campaign of partnerships: between private sector initiative and government, which supported and championed the campaign; among a group of entrepreneurs who led and sustained it; with the corporate world and over sixty businesses who pledged services in support of the campaign at launch.

In less than two months a small group of entrepreneurs went from a chance meeting to working at the heart of government and launching a national campaign which would reach thousands of aspiring and early-stage entrepreneurs.

If the initiative to set up that first meeting, make the initial connection, had not happened, neither would the campaign have emerged and grown. Running your own business or in a busy professional career, your diary soon becomes a pile-up of competing engagements and the temptation is to clear the decks to carve out precious time to focus on the tasks at hand.

But there is a difference between what is urgent and what is merely important. The risk in an overly clinical approach to managing your time is that you will turn down the meeting or opportunity that could lead somewhere new and exciting. For campaigners, every new connection and meeting is just one such potential opportunity. Grab hold of what comes your way: it could be the making of you and your business.

Building Your Network

Oli Barrett has been described by no less than *Wired* as 'the most connected man in Britain', a consummate networker who is known and respected throughout the UK enterprise scene and who has been instrumental in the creation of enterprise campaigns ranging from StartUp Britain to Tenner, which gives schoolchildren a £10 seed fund to create and run a miniature business over the course of a month. We asked him about the secrets of getting an idea off the ground and building a business network:

1. Inspiration
When you boil it all down, campaigners have something they want to change. That could be anything from a law, to a behavioural habit, to something about the country they live in.

I had always wanted to change the way schools taught enterprise and entrepreneurship and thought things were too passive, the kids were just invited to sit and listen to a talk or a lecture. I happened to read about a vicar in Suffolk who had got his congregation being entrepreneurial for him; his idea was to hand out a tenner to each member of his congregation and they had surprised him by turning it into thousands of pounds. That was the inspiration behind Tenner.

2. Distillation

Start by framing your idea in an infectious, catchy, simple way, so when someone writes back they say, 'I love it.' You're always looking for the word love; I love this, I want to help you. That's step one. Make it sound immensely catchy, and I don't mean gimmicky, but it's got to really zing in a sentence: what's the problem worth solving and how are you going to solve it?

3. Connection

Then share the idea. In some cases as widely as possible, though my own preferred method is to convene a small, trusted group initially. I host small events and bring together people I know and trust and ask for their help and support.

4. Recommendation

Don't be afraid to ask people to compliment the idea at an early stage, in writing, and get their permission to share that. I asked Lord Bilimoria [founder of Cobra Beer] to say what he thought about Tenner and with his permission I shared what a great idea he thought it was. That gives credibility, and power.

What influencers are looking for is a sense that you're not alone in this, that you've got cred, traction, momentum they can get behind. That's really important. That might be evidencing the thing you want to change and that gives a level of confidence even though you're very small and just starting out.

5. Determination

Don't be afraid to write to people completely out of the blue who are often very busy. More often than not, when I've met campaigners it's something they've become very good at.

Start practical with the people you know and start big with your ideas, then write to people out of the blue. I wrote to the editor of Newsnight *who I had never met, who had never heard of me; he wrote straight back, asking what I was up to, at which point I replied saying we were doing this crazy scheme called Tenner.*

That was a successful approach because it was well written, brief, complimentary (making direct reference to something that had just gone out on his show); it was very well timed, because it went out just after the show had finished, not as it was on deadline, and it was personalized.

Important people have gatekeepers but well-written messages still get through. The other thing I've learned is you have to write to people more than once. Very often the real breakthrough emails I've had have come through sending something a third or fourth time and not being afraid to do that. Secretly you're sending a message about yourself and your cause, to that person, that it is something you really care about.

6. Vindication

When I was a student I needed some advice about advertising, which I didn't know anything about. I didn't know whether I was allowed to use the names of celebrities on the posters of my student company.

I thought, I don't know anything about advertising, the only name I knew was Saatchi & Saatchi, so I called up their headquarters in London and weirdly got through to their global marketing director, who was immensely engaging and asked me to come and see him. I went down to Saatchi's HQ, which led to three things: meeting their clients at a specially organized event, meeting a financier who secured us £300k of investment, and it led to them giving us our own little office in Saatchi's HQ.

7. Dedication

Constantly help the people in your network, then you'll never be in debt. If all you do, all day, is try and help people, they'll constantly think of you as a helpful individual. It's an exercise in generating and maintaining goodwill. The trick is doing that across 1,000 people and not a dozen. To do that you have to come up with much, much better techniques to keep in touch with people.

Takeaways

- Campaigners realize that the viability of their businesses rests on their ability to build new relationships, and that it is their network that makes them powerful;
- It is essential that you take advantage of the networking opportunities that already exist, but you also need to seize people's attention by making your own mark, be that speaking at an industry event or throwing a party;
- For campaigners, every new connection and meeting is just one such potential opportunity. Grab hold of what comes your way: it could be the making of you and your business.

8

Story

Tell me a fact and I will learn,
Tell me a truth and I will believe,
But tell me a story and it will live in my heart forever.

Indian Proverb

As we have seen, the front line of business today is the battle for attention. Developing trust with your customers, creating a culture that liberates your people and building assiduous networks, are all essential elements in the campaigning armoury: how you harness your mission to best effect to break through. But there is a trump card in getting noticed. To stand out, you need a story.

To cut through the noise, you can hark back to the most ancient techniques of all – to create meaningful connections through the way you talk about yourself and your business. Because however advanced the technological channels may have become, what holds water is still the oldest means of communication there is: storytelling.

Stories are what connect us on an emotional level, inspiring belief in customers who have more reason than ever to be cynical. Why? Because in a complex world where people feel bombarded from all sides, stories offer the precious elixir of simplicity. It is what the Saatchi brothers coined as the 'brutal simplicity of thought': either you can make an instant connection with people based on something immediately identifiable, or they will move on. 'The strongest brands are defined by their ownership of one thought,' Maurice Saatchi told the *Financial Times* in 2006. 'The very strongest by one word.'

A story is what gives you that connection. Either people buy your story, or they start shopping with your competitors. And if the story doesn't stack up, no amount of reasoned evidence will bring them back. The leaders we have met are often defined by their start-up story: a legend that has become defining and which endures.

In business, the story of your early days can set the journey ahead for years to come. When we launched our business, one of the best pieces of advice we received was to keep a diary of our first 100 days. Only much later was it clear just how important capturing those early memories and experiences would be. The living history of your company helps shape your culture, your decisions and the way you communicate with the market at large. It is something that can act as a rallying point for employees and customers alike.

Even businesses that achieve great success will often have founding stories full of jeopardy and near-disaster. Take Evernote, now a billion-dollar company operating out of Silicon Valley, but as recently as 2008 on the brink of winding up.

'We had two weeks of cash left in the bank, it was 3 a.m. and I decided finally, this is it. I'm going to shut down the company tomorrow morning. I'm going to go to sleep, force myself to sleep, come into the office tomorrow, lay everyone off and shut down the company.' So said Phil Libin, the company's founder, speaking to the Y Combinator Startup School in 2013. At 3.10 a.m., an email arrived, from an Evernote fan in Sweden writing to express his love for the product and, as chance would have it, 'to see if you guys need any investment'.

This was October 2008, after months of failing to secure a significant funding round, with the planned lead investor having pulled out on the day of closure, the same day that Lehman Brothers collapsed and the markets began to crash with it. It was 'arguably the worst time to be [fundraising] in the history of the universe'.

Libin never got to bed that night. But half an hour later, he was on a Skype call to the 'random guy in Sweden' and a fortnight later, in receipt of the $500,000 investment that would save the business. Evernote has since become a member of the billion-dollar start-up club and one of Silicon Valley's most valuable tech companies, with over 100 million users around the world.

From near-destruction to a chance email that saved the company and kicked off a rapid phase of expansion. And exactly how this hugely successful founder chooses to tell the tale of his own business, beginning with how it almost failed completely. It is a story that connects, with which people can identify and which can endear buyers and investors alike. Every business has its own: a story defines a business and one of the most important things you can do is learn to nurture and tell your own.

Happily Ever After

A great story needs a great first line. For campaigners it is often this: 'I want to change the world.' The campaigner's story tends to be epic, not just about nudging along and meeting annual growth figures, but standing in front of the bathroom mirror telling yourself that what you are about to do is transformative. The urge to change the world is counter-cultural to a great many people, who would blush at the very notion. But put yourself into a room of entrepreneurs, and such inhibitions fall away. We have attended numerous pitching events in the last few years, from Mile End Road to St James's Palace. One thing you rarely encounter is self-doubt: usually it is ranks of the optimistic, convinced of the validity of their business mission and their own ability to maximize the commercial opportunity they have identified.

Put another way, entrepreneurs know how to tell a good story about themselves. That is true for one simple reason. Namely, at the outset, a story is all a founder has. It is your one and only chip when you make that first pitch – and there is only you to tell it. When you start out, there is no marketing department to outsource to, no one else who can take responsibility for delivering a compelling story that will get the business noticed.

We have heard it said that a start-up is akin to a hypothesis. A founder is taking a considerable bet and asking employees, suppliers and customers to join them in a leap of faith. With little or no physical assets to speak of, your collateral has to be emotional: a story that manifests your ideas, values and promise into something believable and worth joining.

As a founder you start out with nothing other than the absolute courage of your convictions: that your product, service or concept can be a game-changer. A story is how you articulate that belief; it is the convincer, and the first person that must buy into it is you. A great story can help you articulate your mission, communicate your promise and connect with your market.

The Protagonist: Shaving Lives

All great stories have a leading act, and entrepreneurs and their teams often cast themselves in the central role: everyday characters who are driven to exceptional feats of commercial invention.

When people buy a brand, they are not only buying a product or a service but also the image it projects and the story it tells. In business, protagonists serve a dual purpose because not only are they the keepers of the message, jealously guarding the values on which their company was built, but they are also the ones who simultaneously project that message to the outside world.

A protagonist shapes their own story and seeks to mould a campaigning team in his or her image. We heard former Manchester United manager Sir Alex Ferguson say once that he liked to see something of himself in the players he worked with. Many entrepreneurs have told us that they like to hire people better than they are, but it doesn't often ring true. To inspire a team, a culture and customers, the protagonist has to remain firmly at the heart of their growth story.

Among UK start-ups of the past two decades, few have been more identifiable with their founder than King of Shaves, the grooming brand created by Will King in 1993 and which he led until stepping away from the business last year.

From its first chapter, the King of Shaves story has had one distinctive narrative ingredient: conflict. 'I believe you've got to have a point to push against,' King told us. 'That can be a rival firm or it can be an idea. The products we pushed against when launching our oils were those shaving foam cans, the ones that leave the rusty marks on the sink.

'For us, it felt like there was a cosy duopoly in the marketplace; there was an arrogance in there that I didn't like.'

Throughout its life, King of Shaves has been defined as a challenger against market titans, notably Gillette, which has 84 per cent of the UK razor market. That David against Goliath struggle has been a central plank of the King of Shaves story, led by its protagonist. From protesting at Speakers' Corner against the 'cost of shaving' ('listeners, lend me your beards') to spoofing runaway hit *The King's Speech* ('we are at war with a common enemy'), the King has consistently and compellingly played the part of the little guy tweaking the nose of his large competitors and stealing a bit of their lunch.

A business that was set up with just £15,000 in seed capital has put a small but definite hole in the market share of a giant, building a foothold of 3 per cent of the UK razor market and 9 per cent of wet shaving products.

That has not come without a good deal of struggle. 'The real battleground is the retail environment,' King says. 'That, for a challenger brand, is where you really realize what you're up against. A dominant [brand] can up the money and marketing spend to keep you out.

'You might be talking to a supermarket about a possible promotion – say a mid-gondola position offering a third or 50 per cent off. You put your bid in, don't hear anything back, and the next thing you know, the dominant firm have got their product in there instead of yours.'

After King of Shaves launched its first razor seven years ago, having initially focused on wet shaving products, 'things got serious with Gillette,' he says. 'Gillette and Wilkinson Sword have pretty much been on deal or on promotion ever since.'

Through all the struggles of building a brand to take on powerhouse competitors – from being locked out of the US after a dispute with a distributor, to having to spend £1 million in legal fees to patent its most recent razor – King of Shaves has retained its profile and reputation as a distinctive, quirky alternative. In no small part that is down to the storytelling capabilities of its founder, a protagonist with the quintessential entrepreneur's story of rage against the machine.

'The idea behind the original brand had come from solving my own shaving problems,' he says. 'I'd found by luck or judgment that other people had the same problems as well. It was a different landscape to today . . . [and] we were the only brand entering the market at the time.

'It meant that we were able to get into a space, and were able to define ourselves as a great product, the person standing up to the multinationals. We were able to grow by word of mouth and luck.'

In his battle against a Goliath whose advertising spend is approximately fifty times his company's annual revenues, King has relied on a range of means to create that word of mouth. From purchasing the shave.com web domain for $35 in 1995, to being the first non bank or building society to raise funding from the public (a £1,000 retail bond, a model since copied by many other small companies), he has found new means to get his message across. And while still CEO, he retained the personal touch, running the company Twitter account himself.

As the protagonist in his own company growth story, King has continued to evangelize an ambitious vision of what the brand can achieve. A favoured reference point is Nokia and its majority share of the global mobile market, wiped out following the advent of the iPhone.

'I'm a big believer in thinking big,' he told us. 'If you think big and end up small, then that's still good. But if you think small and end up minuscule, then you're in trouble. An entrepreneur thinks it is impossible and I will do it. That's the mindset.' The story he has told over the more than twenty years of his company's development has been a vital part of ensuring that the reality can match at least some of the towering ambition.

The Fundamentals of Telling Your Story

Campaigners may be the ultimate storytellers but the power of narrative is by no means their unique preserve. Story is an asset that can be harnessed by all, from an ambitious individual to a floundering corporation. You must begin by getting your mission right, then storytelling comes in as a major part of the campaigning toolkit, helping you grab attention and generate momentum. But what actually makes for a great start-up story? It must possess a beginning, a middle and an end, but we've also found that it must achieve three main things. These are:

1. Keep it Simple

Leonardo da Vinci said that simplicity is the ultimate sophistication. It should be a poster on the wall of every boardroom in the country. Because while your business story may be a glorious epic in its scale or ambition, at heart it will evoke a glorious simplicity.

Simplicity is the starting point of every good story, and that is the hardest thing to find: the basic essence to convey an authentic truth about your business that people can believe in. When what you have to say is as important as what you have to sell, the story and the ease with which it can be communicated are paramount.

Frank Meehan, partner at SparkLabs Global, has backed successful tech companies around the world, from Siri to Spotify and Summly. He told us that 'simplicity is the absolute key' to a successful pitch to investors. 'If the idea can be explained immediately, that's the winner. Like Snapchat: disappearing messages.

'In terms of the technology itself, there are always at least four or five others in the early stages of doing something similar, so the question is how simple can they make it and how fast can they do it?'

In the 1960s, Kelly Johnson was the lead engineer at Lockheed Skunk Works, the aviation company responsible for building a number of spy planes for the US government. When working on one particular project, Johnson gave his design engineers a bunch of tools to play with. His team might have been brilliant designers, but what they designed, he told them, had to be repairable by a regular mechanic with these tools. In a combat situation, that might be all the equipment available.

To help his designers remember this, Johnson came up with an acronym: KISS. Keep it simple stupid. The same principle was the guiding light of Bill Clinton's 1992 campaign for the US presidency, which constantly brought its pitch to America back to three fundamental storylines: change vs more of the same; the economy, stupid; and don't forget healthcare.

If you can seal your narrative with a KISS, then you'll be well ahead of most of your competition.

2. Be Remarkable

One thing your story must absolutely achieve is to distinguish you from the crowd. We live at a time when choice has never been in greater supply, so standing out demands something better than good. As Seth Godin wrote in *Purple Cow*, 'Something remarkable is worth talking about. Worth noticing. Exceptional. New. Interesting. It's a Purple Cow. Boring stuff is invisible, it's a brown cow.'

To become remarkable, you have to capture people's attention, and an element of risk is often central to that. The Black Farmer founder Wilfred Emmanuel-Jones likes to talk about the importance of jeopardy in a great business story. 'The key thing was coming up with a name,' he has said of his own start-up story. 'There were no black people in Devon and my neighbours were all calling me the Black Farmer and it all stemmed from there.

'I wanted to copy Richard Branson when he launched the Virgin brand, when at the time it was risqué to say the word 'virgin' in public. The name the Black Farmer had a similar effect.'

Being remarkable can be as much about how you communicate as what you are trying to say. Jim, now Lord, O'Neill, the former Goldman Sachs chief economist who coined the now universally used 'BRIC' acronym to highlight the economic potential of emerging markets, told us that the idea only really started to catch on once it had been visualized in terms of future potential. 'For the first couple of years hardly anybody paid any attention to it,' he says. 'It wasn't until we were able to plot out what the world would look like by 2050, which we did two years [after the initial paper] that it started to get more interest. And then very quickly, around 2004–5, it snowballed.' As he relates, an idea that began with a research paper then became a formal political grouping between the nations (Brazil, Russia, India, China and South Africa), which meets annually, and has spawned specialist investment funds and university courses all over the world. The 'branding power' of the BRIC concept, as O'Neill describes it, gave four (latterly five with the inclusion of South Africa) economies a shared dynamism and sense of momentum that has allowed them to set much of the global economic debate in the almost fifteen years since the acronym was coined. It gave them a story to tell.

Suitably crafted and engagingly told, your story is what can make you stand out from a field of sameness and attain the nirvana of being singular, noticeable. It can make you a brand worthy of remark.

3. Make the Connection

Your story must be simple and worthy of remark, but a distilled and distinctive narrative alone will not necessarily do the job. What your start-up story must do above all is make an emotional connection with your customer. It is this quality that is key to creating a great brand that people will want to buy into. Why? Because it unlocks the promise of a better future.

After all, do we really ever buy a car merely to get us from A to B? A pair of trainers to run around the park? A computer to allow us to type? Or do we buy a Bentley or Ferrari to feel more prestigious, Nike to improve our athletic endeavour and Apple to make us cooler and smarter?

Such are the basic human emotions that these brands inspire in us. These are not facts, but beliefs. It helps construct the narrative that we build around ourselves through the consumption of their products.

We have always been very struck by a book called *The Naked Ape*, by the sociologist Desmond Morris. He outlined a series of fundamental human drivers that explain our essential behaviours. Comprising sex, curiosity, prestige and power, winning, health, tribalism, parenthood and protection, these impulses drive our behaviours and decision-making. They provide a map of the mind, and great brands, and indeed great people, tap into and feed those sensibilities. Your business story needs to access that fundamental layer of human emotion if it is to truly break through.

Putting Pen to Paper

Stories are so important in business because they create an emotional connection: with customers, investors, even employees. A story should be the living embodiment of the purpose and promise underpinning the company, one that grows over time but fundamentally never strays too far from the founding principles. The story is a fundamental part of how you unfold your commercial mission and start to build it into a campaign that connects with people.

Your story is also a discipline, one that needs to be captured and understood so that it can be told consistently and to best effect. That makes wordsmiths essential: the artisans in an information age. To shape your story to best effect, you need to write it down and in doing so, take into account four central considerations. These are:

1. The customer
The story needs to follow and speak the language of the customer. What do they like and what influences them? What higher need can you appeal to and how do you make them want to feel part of the same club?

2. The competition
Who are your competitors and how can you differentiate yourself from them? What are they doing well and what are they doing badly? Know and understand the rules of the market before you seek to break them.

3. The campaign
What is the mission behind the business? What was it created to achieve, enable or inspire? This must be a powerful statement justifying your existence in a field likely crowded with competitors and appealing to the instinctive desire of people to be part of something meaningful.

4. The commitment

Your promise to the market: a clear commitment that follows from the mission statement and forms your bond of trust with the customer.

Only by writing down your story can you begin to relate it back to the people with whom it needs to resonate: your customers.

Nurturing Your Story

In an established business, the start-up story is often something that has got lost along the way. In our professional careers, both of us have encountered grown-up companies who have seen their story as something that should only concern the marketing and PR department.

Yet story affects the entire company and is central to how you deliver, sell and grow as a business. It is the manifestation and articulation of the purpose that binds employees and consumers alike to a successful brand. Without narrative, customer loyalty, financial drive and employee motivation are all at risk.

But in a fog of acquisitions, demergers and corporate musical chairs, it is all too easy to lose sight of the story that made a company stand out in the first place. The truth is you are never too old, experienced or well established to ignore your story, or for a founder or CEO to bypass the role of communicator-in-chief.

That status bestows significant influence but also a great responsibility: to be an ambassador for the brand

and company at large. The narrative of your business cannot be outsourced and the chief storyteller must be at the apex of the organization.

A story also extends well beyond the words you use to tell it. Indeed, according to research from Albert Mehrabian, emeritus professor of psychology at the University of California, when people are judging someone speaking to them for the first time, just 7 per cent of their liking is determined by words, and 93 per cent by tone and body language.

It rings true, because as anyone who has frequented pitch situations in their working life will tell you, everything about someone tells a story: from the suit they are wearing to the way they present, their manner and style in addressing you and all manner of body language.

This means you need to kit yourself out, act and present as you would like others to see you. To treat every meeting and new conversation as a chance to hone and project your story.

Also important are the different channels through which you communicate your story. We asked John Cridland, director-general of the CBI, how he maintains a central focus to his organization's campaigning work, when it encompasses so many different and varying elements.

His answer was his business card. 'On the back of one of these business cards there are five CBI pledges,' he told us. 'They are under the theme of delivering prosperity for Britain. In a campaigning organization you have to have an arrowhead which absolutely sums up to the man and woman on the Clapham Omnibus what your piece of the pie is, what your campaign themes are.'

That simplicity is vital because a business can only connect and become meaningful if people are willing to give it the time of day. And the more complicated your message, the less likely that becomes. Campaigners stand out because their purpose is singular and the story that substantiates it is equally straightforward and compelling. The story is what brings a business to life, and yours must be as easy for others to relate to as it is for you to tell. If you can distil your purpose and story on to a standard-size business card, then you won't be going far wrong.

Takeaways

- If business is about a battle for attention, then your start-up story can set you apart from the competition;
- For a fledgling entrepreneur, their story is all they have. It's the only asset they possess to take to investors and to the market. Do not underestimate its value;
- A powerful story will connect emotionally with other people. It must be simple, remarkable and connect with people on an emotional level. It should also consider the customer, the competition, the campaign and show the founder's commitment to the cause;

- A 'start-up' story is not just for start-ups. The story of a business is critical to its success at any stage of its development;
- If you believe your business is losing its way, distil your mission and story to just a couple of sentences to focus everyone's attention.

9

The Communicator-in-Chief

They may forget what you said, but they will never forget how you made them feel.

Carl W. Buehner

'We shall go on to the end, we shall fight in France, we shall fight on the seas and oceans, we shall fight with growing confidence and growing strength in the air, we shall defend our Island, whatever the cost may be, we shall fight on the beaches, we shall fight on the landing grounds, we shall fight in the fields and in the streets, we shall fight in the hills; we shall never surrender . . .'

Fifty years after his death, it is worth considering the famous words of Winston Churchill, someone whose leadership during the Second World War is often remembered through the prism of the speeches he gave to Parliament and the nation. Not just a Commander-in-Chief, Churchill was the archetypal Communicator-in-Chief, someone who knew the power of words to comfort, connect and inspire.

Where the Communicator-in-Chief seems natural enough in the world of politics and government, the role is equally central to the campaigning business. The simple truth for those in business is that your story is no good if there is no one able to do it justice. In a world where companies seek mass belief as much as mass consumption, the importance of communication has become paramount, the means by which campaigning companies stand out. Just as general elections in the UK have become ever more presidential, so business leaders are increasingly the personification of the brands that they represent. If you run a firm your face has a value. And your ability to pitch its personality is a major part of the business's ability to get heard. You would be wrong to think this is a matter of mere celebrity; it is a crucial part of the survival armoury of any business and if you don't use it you lose it.

That's why today's CEO needs a new job spec and that should include the title of Communicator-in-Chief. In this chapter we will look at how business leaders can act as the custodian and champion of their company's story: the bards who take the message to the masses.

Communication Matters

Throughout history we have celebrated leaders with that command of language, that ability to inspire. Shakespeare's Henry V at Agincourt: 'Once more unto the breach, dear friends.' Nelson at Trafalgar: 'England expects every man to do his duty.' Churchill on El Alamein:

'It is not even the beginning of the end. But it is, perhaps, the end of the beginning.'

Wonderful words, dexterously delivered. Surely in this age of instant information we would continue to champion the role of the communicator? Not by any means, as it happens.

Too many senior business people seem to want to discount the importance of communication and its critical effect on leaders and the organizations they head up. There is often a near antagonism towards the expectation that a talent for brilliant communication should be part of the everyday job spec of a CEO or founder.

Part of it is a profound cultural mistrust of slick speakers; new age salesmen with superfluous skills. This is most often personified in the modern mind by politicians but is increasingly an issue for our business leaders.

Another element is a sense that these skills somehow provide an unfair advantage over those whose work should speak for itself. The reflection here is that the communicator by contrast lacks depth and substance.

Often, the point will be made that a great many leading figures have struggled in the limelight, or positively avoided it. That is held as adequate reason to negate its importance.

There is nothing insubstantial about the ability to communicate. Far from it, it is part of the territory. Leaders are expected to use words to defend and advance with all of the vigour and skill of the military leader.

A major part of this is due to advances in technology,

which have amplified the importance of two key factors: transparency and connectivity. Transparency means that there is an ever-greater need to explain because customers know more, want to find out more, and have the tools to discover more at their disposal. Connectivity means that customers behave in an ever more tribal manner. If you are not part of the conversation, you are not part of the sale.

The battlefield is replete with victims who got it wrong. Take Nick Buckles of G4S or the global consulting firm Arthur Andersen. Both spectacularly failed to make their case in the court of public opinion and paid the price.

In a business landscape where intangible assets dominate, communication has assumed a great commercial importance. For instance, researchers estimate that from 2008 the US pharmaceutical industry began spending almost twice as much on promotion as it does on research and development.

Make no mistake, communication matters. Difficult to value it might well be, but it is one of a range of factors that determine the worth of businesses today. It is everywhere and its effects are ubiquitous.

Lessons for Business

Great campaigning leaders keep things fresh. They keep their organizations young even as they grow and diversify. They inspire a growth spirit that is as much an asset of the heart as the head – appealing to employees, customers, investors and advocates. They prioritize how people feel, about themselves and the company, above their position in the pecking order, their role, their earnings.

Jack Welch was a corporate leader who instinctively got the idea of the Communicator-in-Chief in his stint at the helm of GE. He said: 'One thing I learned during my years as CEO is that perception matters. And in these times when public confidence and trust have been shaken, I've learned the hard way that perception matters more than ever.'

It's a tough job spec, and one that requires ever more from leaders. The idea of the campaigning CEO is increasingly the expected and not an exception. Increasingly the leaders of business must follow the communication-led example of their political peers, as the commercial sphere becomes subject to the same kinds of pressures as the traditional election cycle.

In a faster-moving environment, where businesses can just as easily ride a momentum wave as be engulfed by one, the only place for leaders to be is out in front. This is a world where your products, intentions and results can be forensically analysed and publicly called into question.

Faced with this torrent, leaders in business have little option but to become the public face and advocate of their brand. Businesses have become public property in the same way politicians have long been accustomed to having their activities scrutinized.

In a transparent world where there is no hiding place, the leader of a business must also become its public figurehead. Campaigning founders and CEOs show how this necessity can be turned to advantage.

The examples that follow demonstrate the power of the Communicator-in-Chief, both at the helm of a start-up and at a corporate behemoth in need of rescue. The Cobra Beer story highlights how a founder can close the credibility gap that every new business faces before it has established its credentials; while Marks & Spencer under Sir Stuart (now Lord) Rose highlights the role of communication for a CEO seeking to drive a major transformation within a well-known brand. In both cases, the leader as Communicator-in-Chief is the main actor in jump-starting a business or idea which others can adopt, take forward and grow.

Business Communicators: the King of Cobra

The natural business communicators are entrepreneurs, the embodiments of the companies they create. As in the case of Cobra Beer and its founder Lord Bilimoria, that may well stem from how their idea came into being in the first place.

The idea behind Cobra, which now sells in over 98 per cent of the UK's Indian restaurants, was first brewed in Bilimoria's student days, when he developed a taste for English ales but found them undrinkable with curry, as he did fizzy European lagers.

'A lot of challenger brands come through a consumer being dissatisfied,' he told us. 'In my case it was wanting to combine the refreshment of a lager and the smoothness of an ale to produce a beer that blends the two, which no one had ever done before.' The frustration or resolution out of which durable business ideas are born provides the perfect basis for franchising and evangelizing the benefits of the new product or service to doubtful buyers and consumers.

At the beginning, that can seem an almost impossible ask: 'You have zero credibility and invariably have no money,' Bilimoria says. 'Nobody knows you, nobody knows your brand, why should somebody finance you, supply you and buy from you when you have zero credibility? The challenge was not having no money, it was constantly getting people to believe in [us].'

In these formative stages of a business, where an idea can take hold or fade into nothing, clarity and strength of communication is key. And who better to campaign on behalf of a brand than the individual who created it? 'I just had such belief in [Cobra]. I really believed I had this differentiated product that would deliver on my promises,' is Bilimoria's reflection.

As he suggests, the ability to sell your product and convince a critical mass of customers is fundamentally dependent on a personal level of conviction in the value and distinctiveness of the brand. 'You've got to have absolute passion, faith and belief in your ideas and your brand. That gives people the faith and confidence to trust you and give you a chance.'

The next challenge is to convert that belief into a

confidence on the part of buyers and influencers – in Cobra's case, the UK's Indian restaurants. How did a qualified chartered accountant and a Cambridge law graduate, ferrying cases of beer in a beaten-up Citroën 2CV, starting out in the depths of a recession, take on the global giants of the drinks industry and establish market share?

In the early days, weaving a narrative about what Cobra could do for its target restaurants was fundamental. Communicating the unseen benefits is key, Bilimoria says. 'A restaurant will sell more Cobra because it goes better with the food and it's smoother to drink, doesn't make you bloated and isn't too bitter.

'Bottom line, you'll sell more beer, commercially it's better for everyone and you've got a happier consumer.'

Creating confidence within the market was another important part of the Cobra sales pitch, again stemming from Bilimoria's confident presentation of his wares. From the beginning he priced Cobra at a pound more per case than its main rival Kingfisher, and mandated a minimum order of five cases from all initial buyers. What's more, he began by selling only to the upmarket Indian restaurants. 'I knew if the top restaurants started selling the product I could use that as a reference to the other restaurants.' The confidence to market Cobra as a premium product for the premium end of the market was what enabled it to grab a foothold that it has since turned into hegemony. Crucial to projecting that sense of self-assurance was the rock-solid belief and ambitious sales strategy of Cobra's founder, a true Communicator-in-Chief on behalf of his own brand, as he remains today.

Top Tips: Lord Bilimoria

1. **Picture your success:** 'To have [a] vision of where you [want] your product to go is really important, to have that vision of creating a product with global appeal. That visionary aspect, I think, is absolutely key, that right at the beginning, when you have zero credibility, you have an idea that is really scalable and a vision of where you want that idea to get to.'

2. **Deploy the brand:** Bilimoria decided that Indian restaurants were always going to be the foundation for Cobra. 'The authentic double-sized Indian beer bottles that Cobra was produced in, worked extremely well in the restaurant environment, by being visible, attracting attention and raising awareness.' That built a strong foundation for the brand based on word-of-mouth recommendations and it was not until eight years after Cobra was founded that it launched its first advertising campaign.

3. **Package it right:** 'Breakthrough brands are continually innovative, so even with [the] packaging you've got to try and stand out and be iconic.' The Cobra bottle was created around a series of icons,

'where each icon tells a story. No consumer
product has ever told its story visually as part of its
packaging before. So you're constantly trying to do
things that are unique, that are innovative, that are
iconic.'

Business Communicators: the High-Street Houdini

When Stuart (now Lord) Rose returned in 2004 to
Marks & Spencer, the company he had first joined as a
graduate trainee in 1972, the grand dame of the British
high street was undergoing one of the most significant
upheavals in its history. Plummeting market share, a
boardroom clear-out and a high-profile takeover attempt
were the context for one of the retail industry's acknowledged turnaround specialists.

Four years later and, before the recession took its toll,
profits were back at the £1-billion mark for the first time in
over a decade. A renewed focus on the core value offer and
a smart advertising campaign played a significant part but
perhaps his most distinctive contribution was a far-reaching
sustainability programme, Plan A. He told us about the
challenges of implementing a campaign mentality into a
business with tens of thousands of employees and with a
123-year history when he announced the plan in 2007.

In his view, the role of the leader as communicator is
essential: 'It's about selling your belief and selling your
ideas, articulating it in a simple way so that it becomes
absolutely tangible to people.'

In a corporate organization with a large staff, clarity and simplicity of message is fundamental, he believes. 'You need to be very, very focused and very, very clear in your communications; you do need to remember that you have got to trickle that down to every single outlet and every single place where these people are.'

The origins of Plan A, which saw a £200-million investment in 100 initial commitments on issues such as supply chain efficiency, sustainable use of energy and packaging reduction, demonstrate how a singular vision from the top of an organization can be the lever for a campaign that effects a tangible change.

'I was looking to set up a way to differentiate the business,' says Lord Rose. 'Often ideas don't come from sitting down and thinking hard about great ideas; you have to go out and they appear to you. I was tired, I was going on holiday, I ran into a bookshop, picked up half a dozen books and one of them was Al Gore's book on climate change, *An Inconvenient Truth*.

'I was very taken by the graph on the front page which is the graph of CO_2 emissions [from 1945] and the graph only [goes up].

'I started researching it and I came back and decided . . . to get the film when it came out. I hired a cinema and I showed the top 100 staff at M&S. I said to them, "We've got to do something about this – we could make a difference here because we're a sustainable company, we're a company that's in touch with our consumers, we've always had a good record in terms of ethical trading." '

The challenge to bring about Plan A was as much one of communication as it was implementation, he says. 'When we started talking about the details of a hundred different things we could do, the two difficult things were selling it internally. We faced scepticism, a lot of scepticism further down in the business. When we said we're going to launch a Plan A, people said, "What's that about? Are people going to come around and tell us to turn switches off?"'

'The second thing was that we were going to tell the investment community we were going to spend over £200 million over five years, without paying a penny back to the consumer. All they could see was that was a £200-million margin spend – why would we want to do that?'

The response to that scepticism was simplicity and consistency of communication, Lord Rose believes. 'You tell people the truth, keep the message simple, keep the people near, keep reporting back how they're doing, and then if you're doing it well, accelerate it. If you're not doing it well, say that it's not working.'

Despite the early doubts, the message held and so too has the worth of the programme. In 2012 the company was able to announce it had become fully carbon neutral, and delivered on the majority of its initial commitments. What's more, within three years Plan A had delivered £50 million of profit that was funnelled back into product development. Under new management, M&S has extended the plan with additional commitments that run until 2020. It has proven an unlikely success that could not have been achieved without the ability of a Communicator-in-Chief to sell a complicated and unfamiliar plan to action to a diverse audience of employees, investors and external interests.

Top tips: Lord Rose

1. **Be half a step ahead:** 'If you're a step ahead of the consumer, you're often too far ahead, if you're in line with the consumer, you're often too far behind. The trick is to be half a step ahead, so that they don't know you want it, until you've put it in front of them.'

2. **Fight for your ideas:** 'I had to fight very hard for [Plan A]. I had to fight hard for it as a company and I had to fight hard for it within the investment community. Although interestingly enough, when you articulate it and you beat the drum for long enough and you're consistent about the messaging, and you've sent that around your organizations; once you've got some traction and the traction has got very strong, it becomes self-fulfilling.'

3. **Beware complacency:** 'Getting momentum is hard, keeping the momentum is easier. The problem seems to be the complacency, greed and sort of arrogance and the sort of CEOs who think they are invincible. That's a very dangerous place.'

Lessons from Government: a Tale of Two Presidents

Business leaders like Lord Rose and Lord Bilimoria show how adept CEOs and entrepreneurs can be at capitalizing on the power of communication to drive their companies forward, be they just starting out or long established. But business still has much to learn from the field of politics, a world that is in many ways akin to a permanent state of start-up. To get anywhere, to do anything, you have to win. From being selected by your own party as a candidate, to standing for office, through to appointment to the great offices of state, everything relies on your ability to beat rivals, have a clearer message, and a sharper mind.

Recent US Presidential elections have provided a treasure trove of techniques for business. From ground-breaking social media campaigns to the ultimate in 'media friendly' candidates, these elections have set the course for business as much as they have for a nation.

There are many skills lurking within the political bubble that can be used to great effect in the commercial arena. If you are in the business of campaigning you have more in common with the leaders of government than you may think.

In the US Constitution it reads that, 'The President shall be Commander-in-Chief of the Army and the Navy of the United States.' For the modern American President, the ability to communicate has become an integral part of the job, one understood in particular by two modern presidents from either side of the political spectrum.

Ronald Reagan, Republican President from 1981 to 1989, was known as the 'Great Communicator' – the Hollywood regular who made it to the White House. His presentational skills were honed from his early days as a sports broadcaster and through a host of dubiously remembered B movies.

Often dismissed as a political lightweight, Reagan was far more than an accomplished actor and radio man transplanted on to the political stage. What made him the archetypal Communicator-in-Chief was an innate ability to turn the complex social, economic and political issues of the day into messages that resonated with his audience; to establish a connection and build the trust that became votes which delivered consecutive election victories, including his 1984 landslide when he carried all but one of the then fifty states.

'You and I have a rendezvous with destiny,' he ended his famous 'A Time for Choosing' speech, in support of 1964 Republican Presidential candidate Barry Goldwater, the oration often seen as his springboard from the worlds of media and cinema into front-line politics. 'We'll preserve for our children this, the last best hope of man on earth, or we'll sentence them to take the last step into a thousand years of darkness.' The stark metaphor, nod to the common territory of family and exaggerated sense of jeopardy add up to a line that is all about impact and connection.

Speaking directly to voters in a way that would be heard was the common thread through Reagan's speeches as a candidate and President. In 'A Time for Choosing', the phrase 'You and I' crops up no less than ten times. Debating Jimmy Carter in 1980, he infamously skewered the incumbent President with a line addressed not to his opponent, but to the television viewers: 'Are you better off now than you were four years ago? Is it easier for you to go and buy things in the stores than it was four years ago? Is there more or less unemployment in the country than there was four years ago? Is America as respected throughout the world as it was?'

Reagan was not the 'Great Communicator' merely by dint of great speech-writing or sound bites, though those are well remembered ('the aggressive impulses of an evil empire'; 'Mr Gorbachev, tear down this wall!').

It was his ability to speak to and not at his audience, 'to educate his audience, to bring his ideas to life . . . to make his arguments vivid to the mind's eye' in the words of his chief speech-writer Ken Khachigian, that distinguished Reagan as a communicator. That allowed him to win, in business terms, an unparalleled customer loyalty and even affection.

Twenty years after he departed the White House, another brilliant communicator took his place in the Oval Office. Barack Obama is a President in a media landscape completely changed from Reagan's time – social media, twenty-four-hours news, the Internet, are just some of the mediums for a modern American leader to master.

And master them, Obama certainly has. In his 2008 campaign, he used the Internet, text and email messages to target young voters, so successfully that he was voted Advertising Age's 'Marketer of the Year'. His campaign had a slogan ('Change we can believe in'), a chant ('Yes we can') and a poster (Shepard Fairey's red, white and blue 'Hope' portrait) that were identifiable, memorable and shareable.

In office, his control of his message continued. 'His first 100 days have been marked by the omnipresence of Obama the communicator,' noted the *Washington Post*. The newspaper also commented that 'most notable about all the words spoken is the variability of their tone, the way in which Obama has modulated his pitch for different moments.'

Even by his re-election in 2012, with much of his trust capital diminished, he could still speak to voters in a way few others could. In his victory speech providing his Churchillian version of the idea of principle, trust and duty he said: 'America's never been about what can be done for us; it's about what can be done by us together, through the hard and frustrating but necessary work of self-government. That's the principle we were founded on.'

At that point, the seduction of hope, the romance of the future, and the generosity of a big-hearted America melted hearts. On that turf it was Obama's to win all the way.

Any entrepreneur or business leader wanting to get their message across could do worse than study these two emblematic political Communicators-in-Chief.

Any business that succeeds by pitching ideas or

products to a customer or client is involved in a process akin to politics. Anyone who sits on a board of directors is involved in a political process. Anyone who speaks on behalf of his or her brand and uses that conversation to build a positive profile from the media through to shareholders is in the vote-winning game.

Both need to demonstrate vision, build belief and exude friendship to succeed. It is for these reasons that a keen appreciation of the political realm can pay important commercial dividends.

Lessons from Government: Lose a Million Pounds

Great stories can capture hearts and minds. But to do that they need equally great communicators. Getting the message out there is about more than slick taglines and cute advertising. Nor is it a weight that can be borne on a single set of shoulders, important as the lead advocate often is. You need people to tell your story – to their friends, colleagues and family. A campaign requires an army of messengers and ambassadors to spread your identity, your product, your vision.

In 2008, the mayor of Oklahoma, Mick Cornett, kicked off a city-wide health and fitness drive for one of the most overweight urban areas in the US. Standing at 180 pounds, he was a curious pin-up for healthy living, but captured minds almost instantly with his clarion call: 'We're going to lose a million pounds.'

Soon the campaign was underway: a website, www.this

cityisgoingonadiet.com, was set up, hosting a giant counter on which the city collectively recorded the poundage it shed. Of around 150,000 overweight Oklahomans, almost 50,000 signed up to the programme.

Around the city, restaurants began offering special low-calorie menus while gyms gave discounts to participants. After just a year and a half the city had dropped 500,000 collective pounds. But Mayor Cornett wasn't satisfied; as far as he was concerned, they were only halfway there.

As with many American cities, in Oklahoma the car is king. In a bid to change the commuter's weapon of choice, the mayor tabled a referendum. The proposal was to introduce a seven-year, one-cent increase in sales tax to pay for bike lanes, sidewalks, hiking trails, ice rinks, green spaces and a wellness centre.

The population responded with a landslide 'yes'. In 2011, Oklahoma dropped its millionth pound.

Mick Cornett's career illustrates the greatest strength that leaders bring to the age of campaigns; their humanity. 'Let's lose a million pounds' could never have been made to succeed by a clever advertising campaign devised by federal bureaucrats. Oklahomans responded to their mayor because he was one of them, because he was a man standing up and saying, 'We have the same problem, let's solve it together.'

It is exactly that human connection that is demanded of leaders in all spheres today. In the nineteenth century, a great figure like Isambard Kingdom Brunel could succeed on the strength of his ambition and ability – as a pure engineer. But to build the same bridges today, he would be expected to be a communicator on behalf of the businesses he represented, to sell the vision that would secure the investment and the stakeholders to make the project happen. Good work does not speak for itself – it requires a storyteller who can bring it to life for audiences who might otherwise never know it existed, or why they need to be a part of it.

You need to be prepared to fight for a toehold in the market, because nobody is going to award it to you based on merit. It is a global battle for ideas, and in this battle the best story wins.

Communication that Connects: Two Lessons from Government

1. Stories connect: Politicians can attract ridicule for being too ready to serve up anecdotes that look suspiciously ready-made. But when a story is both authentic and ambitiously told, woven into the wider narrative of a campaign, its ability to resonate is unparalleled. Barack Obama's breakthrough speech, to the Democratic National Convention in 2004, began not with a political statement but a family history.

'My father was a foreign student, born and raised in a small village in Kenya. He grew up herding goats, went to school in a tin-roof shack. His father, my grandfather, was a cook, a domestic servant to the British. But my

182

grandfather had larger dreams for his son. Through hard work and perseverance my father got a scholarship to study in a magical place, America, that's shown as a beacon of freedom and opportunity to so many who had come before him.'

And so he continued. From the disparate origins of his parents Obama was quickly able to weave a narrative of opportunity, personal journey and freedom and bind his own story to that of the quintessential American dream. That value of personal narrative and history is as relevant in business as it is in politics; your story and how you tell it is crucial to obtaining the attention, trust and loyalty of customers and employees alike.

2. Slogans sell: Successful political leaders are often remembered by pronouncements of no longer than five words ('Yes we can', 'It's the economy, stupid', 'Education, education, education', 'The lady's not for turning'). It's no different in business, and if you can't sum up the essential worth of your company in a slogan succinct enough to fit on the proverbial political bumper sticker, you probably don't understand it well enough yourself.

Totemic companies are as identifiable by their core slogans as political leaders: the architects of 'Just do it', 'Think different' and 'Every little helps' need no introduction. It may not be inscribed on billboards across the world's biggest cities, but the mantra that underpins your business is no less important to your chances of success. No more than five words: write it down.

Takeaways

- This is a world where people won't buy from you unless they believe in you – and communication is the route to achieving it. Every campaigner, entrepreneur or chief executive must become the Communicator-in-Chief of their business;
- Being a Communicator-in-Chief means telling your start-up story in a compelling way to gain followers and inspire your employees to get behind your cause. In fact, the greatest strength that leaders can bring during the age of campaigns is their humanity;
- In large organizations, simplicity and consistency of message is king, communicating concepts in a way that can be universally understood and adopted;
- There is much business can learn from politics. Like presidents or prime ministers, business leaders are increasingly the personification of the brands that they represent. If you run a firm, your face has a value, so you must become your company's public advocate;
- Businesses can learn the concept of momentum from the political sphere. Are you losing or gaining ground?

IO

Failure

Everybody has a plan until they get punched in the mouth.
Mike Tyson (allegedly)

There is nothing like the spectre of failure to test the strength of mission. Almost all business figures, however successful, will have been faced at some point by the prospect of serious failure. Take Sir Charles Dunstone, one of Britain's most successful self-made men. The UK's first digital billionaire, he co-founded Carphone Warehouse with £6,000 in 1989 and, in 2014, took it into a £3.6-billion merger with Dixons.

But when we listened to him tell his business story, one phrase stood out, delivered with tongue in cheek, but a salient point nonetheless. It was the phrase he said he wanted inscribed on his headstone, one to signify the hand-in-hand relationship between success and failure. The five words were: 'He got away with it.'

In one short sentence he captured the least told chapter in the life story of many great campaigners. That failure, and the fear of it, is every bit the co-pilot of success.

The idea of the entrepreneur as an untroubled winner is more myth than reality. Every business, however strong and enduring its mission, will face significant challenges: the fear of cash flow out of control, not being paid, not winning a contract; the cost of a life where family, friends and loved ones can be the ultimate sacrifices.

And for every inspiring success story of triumph against the odds, there are a great many more tales of failure, of lives where luck ran out. The majority of businesses end in failure: only one third of firms started today will make it through to their third birthday.

According to Aston Business School, of all the UK small businesses started each year, only 10 per cent will still be in existence ten years later. House of Commons statistics published in 2013 showed that 'there were 261,000 business births in 2011 and 230,000 business deaths.'

A business is a fragile cargo and in the vulnerable start-up phase you are frequently confronted by peril. The roster of successful founders with a business failure on their CV is almost endless, from Henry Ford to Bill Gates and Sir Richard Branson.

Failure, however great or small, is an inevitable part of building something; it is a learning experience which helps you to craft and none your mission. For some, it will come in doses small enough to be rendered a survivable mishap. And what doesn't put you out of business will probably make you tougher and more prepared for the next bump in the road.

Mike Tyson once said: 'Everybody has a plan until they get punched in the mouth.' But it was a fellow (if fictional) pugilist, Rocky Balboa, who captured best of all the mindset of the campaigner when it comes to confronting and overcoming failure.

'The world ain't all sunshine and rainbows. It's a very mean and nasty place and I don't care how tough you are. It will beat you to your knees and keep you there permanently if you let it. You, me, nobody is gonna hit as hard as life. But it ain't about how hard you hit. It's about how hard you can get hit and keep moving forward. How much you can take and keep moving forward. That's how winning is done.'

Or consider another cultural icon, Eminem. 'Success is my only mother****ing option' was his memorable take on the matter, a mindset shared by many in business. Campaigners are defined not by the experience of failure but the response to it. It's a simple equation: either you get the better of a bad situation or it gets the better of you. This is when the campaigner's skill set comes into its own: vision to see past the blockage, the willingness to innovate your way out of a problem and the energetic optimism to power you through.

That's why Dunstone's words struck a chord with us: failure is never too distant a cousin to progress and the growth of your business; to succeed you need to know what the better end of a tussle with fate feels like. And if a campaigner is equipped above all for one thing, it is to ride the challenges and hazards that emerge on the horizon of any company or career.

'If': the Poetry of Entrepreneurship

Rudyard Kipling's 'If' must count as the ultimate entrepreneur's poem:

> If you can meet with Triumph and Disaster
> And treat those two impostors just the same . . .

So many entrepreneurs we have met love this poem. It symbolizes the relationship between inspiration and desperation that sums up the start-up and growth experience.

Failure for the entrepreneur is a fear that is total and singular in definition: the destruction of your dream and all you have strived to build. It is a potent and portentous confrontation with mortality. It is perhaps the spectre of failure that drives the fearlessness of the true campaigner, the obsessive survivor who sees life in the most vivid and subjective of terms. Who may see what others term a life of achievement as one of unfulfilled ambitions.

Those with the ambition, desire and belief that they can change things for the better are also the tribe most haunted by the possibility that they might fail in the endeavour. Make no mistake; the fear of failure is a major part of the outlook of some of the most successful people in this country. It is a complex, painful and highly nuanced issue.

But as Kipling suggests, failure is not a finality. The big question is not what it does to you, but rather what you will do in return.

If necessity is said to be the mother of invention, then for some of the world's most successful business leaders, failure has been important enough to claim shared parentage. Take the story of one of Britain's most successful product launches in recent years: James Dyson's bag-free vacuum cleaner.

Dyson got the original idea for the product back in the late 1970s. He'd bought what was meant to be the most powerful vacuum cleaner on the market. But he quickly realized that, along with every other vacuum, there was a design flaw in how it had been put together: 'It was essentially useless. Rather than sucking up the dirt, it pushed it around the room.'

Dyson had come across a different concept in a sawmill, where a cyclonic separator was used to remove dust from the air. If he could use the same principle on a vacuum cleaner, Dyson realized, he had the germ of something potentially exciting.

That, though, was the late 1970s. The bagless Dyson DC01 didn't reach the UK market until 1993. In between, there were a lot of prototypes: over 5,000 in fact. But as Dyson told *Fast Company* in 2007: 'I made 5,127 prototypes of my vacuum before I got it right. There were 5,126 failures. But I learned from each one.'

It would have been easy for Dyson to give up on his idea: 'By the time I made my fifteenth prototype, my third child was born. By 2,627, my wife and I were really counting our pennies. By 3,727 my wife was giving art lessons for some extra cash.'

Yet as he told *Management Today* in 1999, he credits the multiple setbacks on the way to the final product as a major part of its eventual success: 'Success is made up of 99 per cent failure. You galvanize yourself and you keep going, as a full optimist . . . hope is the most important element in success.'

Dyson's vacuum cleaner design had come a long way from the early versions made out of cardboard and duct tape. But even then, he still faced an uphill battle to get it to market. Trying to persuade a mail-order catalogue to be his first customer, Dyson was asked, 'Why should I take a Hoover or an Electrolux out of the catalogue to put in yours?' Dyson's response was, 'Because your catalogue is boring.' The buyer told him he was 'cheeky' but became his first customer.

Later, Dyson's hard work was rewarded with a huge stroke of luck. In 1995, Lord Howe, the former Foreign Secretary, was being shown round the factory. A comment from Dyson that he was struggling to get the vacuum cleaner into the retailer Comet led to Howe responding, 'My wife's on the board!' The following day, Dyson had the purchasing director on the phone. Twelve months later, he had the biggest selling vacuum cleaner in the UK and today Dyson is a multi-billion pound company with over 4,000 employees.

'When it comes to failure,' Dyson wrote in 2011, 'I'm

trumped by [Thomas] Edison who famously said, "I have not failed. I've just found 10,000 ways that won't work." Those 10,000 detours resulted in the Dictaphone, mimeograph, stock ticker, storage battery, carbon transmitter and his joint invention of the lightbulb. In the end, 10,000 flops fades into insignificance alongside Edison's 1,093 patents.'

Failure: on Your Terms

If for an inventor like Dyson, the sum of many failures ultimately built the road to success, for another notable British entrepreneur, setbacks have been something more to steamroller than build upon.

In 1998, Sir Richard Branson drove a Sherman tank into New York's Times Square. The way in was littered with Coca Cola and Pepsi Cola cans, which Branson gleefully crushed in what he hoped would become a metaphor for his new product launch. Keeping up the theme, he then took aim at the famous Coca Cola sign, before revealing a forty-foot billboard above the Virgin Megastore.

This was the US launch of Virgin Cola, Richard Branson's attempt to take on the 'duopolists' of Coke and Pepsi. Branson had created the product alongside a Canadian soda maker, the Cott Corporation, and had high hopes of success. He'd taken on British Airways and the vested interests of the airline industry. So why not Coke and Pepsi?

Branson believed he had a better tasting product than

his two bestselling rivals — it was sweeter tasting and less gassy, making it both a better mixer and also more refreshing to drink.

He also had a bottle modelled on one of the best known celebrities of the time: the curves of the 'Pammy', as the bottle became known, were meant to echo the figure of *Baywatch* star Pamela Anderson.

Yet for all these positives, Branson lost. And lost big. Coca Cola's response to Branson was to double its budget for advertising and marketing. In the US, Virgin Cola failed to get a foothold in the market. In the UK, Virgin Cola's market share stalled at just 3 per cent. Pretty soon, the only places you could buy Virgin Cola were on a Virgin train or a Virgin plane. In 2009, the drink was finally pulled.

The failure of Virgin Cola was a high-profile disaster for Branson. When you've driven a tank into Times Square to launch a product, there's not really anywhere to hide when things go wrong. But it was not a one-off mishap.

There was the Virgin Vodka to mix your Virgin Cola with. Or maybe a glass of Virgin Vines wine to go with your supper? Or if you're feeling tired, how about a Virgin Energy Shot or a bottle of Virgin Ooze?

If you wanted to get married in the late 1990s, you could go to Virgin Brides for your wedding dress (launched, of course, with Branson dressed up as a bride-to-be). Then there was Virgin's briefly lived lingerie range — Virginware (launched this time, thankfully, without Branson's modelling skills).

Remember Virgin Cars? Not many people do: between 2000 and 2003, the firm sold just 12,000 vehicles. Or how about the cosmetics brand Virgin Vie or his Virgin Clothing company? Virgin Pulse – Branson's alternative to iTunes? VirginStudent, an early noughties answer to Facebook? Virgin Express, the low-cost airline to rival EasyJet?

Any which way you look at it, the history of Virgin is littered with businesses that didn't make it. They're not alone in this: we could have made a similar list of Apple flops (the Apple Lisa? The Newton MessagePad? The Pippin Games Console?). Indeed, every successful campaigner company in this book will have some similar sort of tale to tell. What is more, despite a raft of superficial commercial failures, we rightly continue to see Branson as a winner. Each discarded venture has been an essential footnote in the creation of a world-class brand, part of its anatomy as a market leader.

Moreover, have Branson's failures changed his attitude towards business? Not a bit of it. Branson knows that he is going to have failures, but carries on anyway. Only by giving your ideas a go can you discover whether they're going to work or not.

Branson, too, knows how failure can deliver success. His first foray into business, the *Student* newspaper back in the late 1960s, was a flop but one decision, almost as an afterthought, was a runaway success: selling records by mail order in the magazine's back pages. The focus shifted, Branson opened his first Virgin record store on Oxford Street, and a business empire was born.

Twenty-five years on and huge success later and Branson was still learning from his mistakes. Virgin Cola might not have succeeded, but there were lessons Branson felt he could take away from the experience.

'The lesson to be learned from [Virgin Cola] was simple. When we've taken on big companies before, like British Airways, we've come up with a product that is far better than them . . . with soft drinks, there's much of a muchness between two soft drinks which taste roughly the same. So when [Coca Cola] tried a dirty tricks campaign to drive us out of business, they succeeded.

'There's no point in going up against a Goliath unless your product is a lot better than the Goliath's. Virgin learned from the Virgin Cola experience to only launch products where we were a lot better than the Goliaths we were up against and to make sure that what we were charging people was very competitive and generally speaking better than the Goliaths.'

Virgin Cola might not have been good business but learning from why it wasn't good business, was. As the campaigner who has treated failure as very much part of the business cycle, Branson has shown that it is not the experience of it that matters, but how you respond in turn. The lesson this can teach is that failure is a subjective term, one whose definition is very much in the hands of the campaigner to determine. Society is often all too quick to cast the aspersion of failure when those in business might think they are on the way to something special. As a campaigner, you can only ever truly fail on your own terms.

Failing Well

As so many successful campaigners show, failure is not just something that can be overcome but often a means of understanding how better to succeed: a central part of refining your mission, understanding how to campaign and build momentum for your business.

Evernote founder Phil Libin, who as we saw earlier almost had to shut down the business he has since built into a billion-dollar entity, has made the argument that the churn of business formation and failure can have a net positive effect:

'For every billion-dollar start-up created in the US, there are 50,000 to 100,000 companies that are born, try to raise venture capital, succeed or fail to various extents and never quite make it,' he has said. 'For a country to make a company that will succeed like Google, it has to make about 100,000 companies that won't. The good news [is] a country gets far more cumulative economic value from the 100,000 companies that don't make it big than from the one that does.'

Often America is held up as an example of a society where the net benefits of business failure are recognized, while the UK is conversely characterized as an unforgiving environment for failure, a place where we lack the maturity to realize that falling off the ladder early might make you stronger for your next attempt.

We met Michael Birch, the founder of Bebo, in California and he put it to us like this: 'Whereas in the US they'd ask what did you learn from [failure], in the UK they would see it as proof that it was a bad idea.'

Betfair founder Ed Wray has frequently expressed similar sentiments: 'The fear of failure is the single biggest thing I think that holds back the [UK's] entrepreneurial culture,' he told the *Daily Telegraph* in 2013. 'The fear of failure, and the criticism of failure.' In his view, 'Failure is a dirty word and we have to de-stigmatize it and encourage people not to be afraid to fail.'

Without doubt, as the stories of Dyson and Branson show, the lessons of failure can be empowering ones for those who avoid being overwhelmed by the experience.

Indeed in some of the world's most successful companies, failure is to some extent hard-wired into the culture: as the prerequisite of success. Facebook's famous creed of 'move fast and break things' is perhaps the ultimate example of where trying new things that may not immediately work is prioritized over getting it right every time.

'As most companies grow, they slow down too much because they're more afraid of making mistakes than they are of losing opportunities by moving too slowly,' Mark Zuckerberg said in a letter to Facebook shareholders in 2012. 'We have a saying: "Move fast and break things." The idea is that if you never break anything, you're probably not moving fast enough.'

Sheryl Sandberg backed this philosophy up, speaking on the *Charlie Rose* show: 'We are not aiming for

perfection that comes over years and then we ship a product . . . we work on things, we ship them, we get feedback
from the people who use it, we get feedback from the
world, we iterate. We have these great signs around,
"Done is better than perfect."'

What this means in practice is that Facebook isn't afraid
to try things: the criticism the site sometimes gets from
users as they find an element of the site altered is part and
parcel of that process. Driven by an urge to retain the
start-up culture of a company founded in a college dor-
mitory, it is happier to see engineers and developers get
something wrong than not try it at all.

Failure becomes not an end but a means: to learning
the lessons and obtaining the insights to get it right the
next time. The experience of failure can be bitter but the
ultimate outcome need not be.

The Quest for Best

The leader of a company or department must be willing
to embrace the possibility of failure in order to succeed,
and the same should apply to how they develop their
team.

In business, getting better is an exhausting process.
The constant pursuit of self-improvement is what gets
you there and that can only happen in an environment
where people are challenged sufficiently that failure
becomes a distinct possibility.

Only by setting the bar high, and continuing to move it

that bit higher than people think they are capable of, does improvement come. It is an ethos summarized eloquently in the words of St Jerome:

Good, better, best
Never let it rest
Until your good is better
And your better, best.

Like many founders, we initially built a team not of seasoned veterans but from young graduates, with a lot of responsibility thrown on their shoulders. We had to put our faith in their ability to deliver, and to face up to the prospect that we might be asking too much. So often that faith was rewarded. That pressure to succeed, the shadow and threat of failure, is often the making of talent, revealing the true character of great people and helping win the day.

When you and your team are looking failure in the eye, you will tend to bring out the best in each other and rise to the occasion. Improvement does not arise from doing the same thing or being faced by the same responsibilities. What is great today may only be good tomorrow and likewise what is challenging now may quickly become routine.

Only through that quest for best, by aspiring to new challenges and successes, do your business and your people improve. And people who are helped to face up to the possibility of failure, and overcome it time and again, are the ones who will get better.

Responding to Failure

For campaigners, it is the response to failure and setbacks rather than the experience of them that is defining. The impulse to hit back twice as hard as you have been hit. The truth is that everyone in business will experience some level of failure, be it the total collapse of a company through to the more common everyday struggles of lost talent and work.

In many circumstances, a failure or setback will also mean an opportunity. That could be a lost piece of business, freeing up time and capacity to pursue something new and better. Or a departed employee, giving the next person down the chance to step into bigger shoes and prove themselves.

Ultimately what failure represents in business is a sudden movement, a shifting of the sands. And as long as the earthquake is not too severe, that presents as much opportunity as it does challenge.

What the campaigner must aspire to is to keep moving. To replace assets or assignments that the business loses – to learn the lessons of poor performance and share the cost of improvement. To work twice as hard to create a new opening that will make up for the door that has been slammed in your face.

Keeping moving is also about staying ahead of the trends and competitors in your market that threaten your survival as an organization. King of Shaves founder Will

King told us that his mantra is 'Embrace change as a constant: You never know what is going to happen, so you need to constantly be thinking, what's going to disrupt us, threaten us, how do we deal with that? You only have to look at BlackBerry or Nokia to realize that if you think you've got it made and can sit back, you're going to end up in trouble.'

Business history is rife with the stories of companies that failed to anticipate the change that precipitated the failure of what appeared a stable company. Or, as in the case of film company Kodak, who saw the change but failed to respond adequately to it. It was a Kodak engineer who built the first digital camera in 1975, but the company chose to avoid going mainstream with a product seen as threatening to its Polaroid and film business. In seeking to shore up its position, Kodak failed to see that it was standing firm on ground that was dissolving beneath its feet.

The lesson of Kodak is that, in a market that presents the threat of constant disruption, ultimate success may only come through accepting the eventual failure of once dominant products and services. Clinging on rather than moving on is what will often be fatal, something apparently recognized by another giant of American twentieth-century technology, Xerox.

Like Google, Xerox was the brand that became a verb, the company inextricably linked with paper printing and copying. Yet that was exactly the market it had to move away from as the digital revolution began to consume its market at the turn of the century and the company share price fell from $64 in May 1999 to $7 in March 2001. A painful ride through the dotcom bubble and the 2008 market crash has seen what could so easily have become a casualty of the Internet era recover its fortunes by developing new service lines well beyond paper and ink. 'Crisis is a very powerful motivator,' Anne Mulachy, the company's CEO from 2001–9 has said. 'It forces you to make choices that you probably wouldn't have made otherwise. It intensifies your focus, your competitiveness, your relentless desire to attain best-in-class status.'

The contrasting experiences of Kodak and Xerox show that failure stalks even those businesses that seem impregnable in their market dominance, and that the response to the threat of change is what matters above all. Imagine if, rather than reinforcing a failing business model, Kodak had managed to reinvent itself as a digital image business. The first-mover advantage of a pre-eminent giant could have taken the market by storm. While momentum in business is difficult to recover once lost, the Xerox story shows it can be done. Setbacks and failure in business will always be what you make of it. And what doesn't stop you in your tracks can't kill you.

Takeaways

- For campaigners, the prospect of failure always stalks the progress and growth of your business;

- Only by giving your ideas a go can you discover whether they're going to work or not. Treat failure as part of the business cycle;
- Encourage a culture of experimentation and creativity within your business, and tolerate a degree of failure;
- Learn from your failures and keep on moving. It will be your attitude towards the mistakes you make that will define you and your business.

11

Growth

*Success seems to be connected with action. Successful people
keep moving. They make mistakes, but they don't quit.*
Conrad Hilton

For campaigning businesses, powered by purpose and
held together by a shared culture and values, the ultimate
test is that of scale. In a company that is growing fast, you
experience everything exponentially, which creates significant structural, attitudinal and emotional pressures.

That is not to downplay either the significance or diffi-
culty of getting a company off the ground. There is
something commercially valiant and death-defying about
the early days of running a business. You make it against
the odds and everything you do for a brief period is a
first. Your first hire, your first win, your first million. The
first 100 days, as you build your identity, mission and reputation, are in many ways the most precious and enjoyable
of all.

The greatest advantage is that when you start a business at the bottom, if you play it right, the only way is up.

Lean, mean and competitive, a young, aggressive start-up can often be the bane of many a larger, bloated rival, weighed down by costs and accumulated baggage. Smaller teams and shorter decision-making processes make for more nimble management practices and keep the business focused and manageable.

But if small is beautiful, ambitious and growing firms face a challenge to maintain the virtues of the start-up phase. Just as a child grows up quickly, so too can your company. Given a fair wind, your bouncing baby business will soon become an altogether more gangling, adolescent firm, with all the growth pains and hormonal surges that brings. And you will recognize a new and unlikely foe, the side effects of growth.

Successful early days put you on the road to the altogether bulkier challenge of your industry's mid-market. The common thread is that you will face a new generation of young firms with their sights firmly fixed on knocking you off your perch, while larger players are likely to look at your lunch as something they want for their own.

Many good businesses get to this stage and buckle. The expectation is that growth and size will provide a level of protection to ease the situation, but in truth the opposite applies. Danger abounds. Maintaining the campaigning spirit of a start-up is the best way of dealing with it, a need that the likes of Facebook have invested heavily in.

The growth pains of business are in achieving scale without losing soul. In keeping mission central to everything that you do and never losing the will to campaign. And as you expand you face the greatest danger for any emerging business: the point when it stops seeing itself as a start-up and loses the entrepreneurial urge, the pioneering spirit.

That is the spirit which inspires people to relentlessly do more, go further and give the very best of themselves. And it is most potent and precious in the early days when the chips are most clearly down.

The start-up culture is about fierce activity, urgently undertaken with the keenest sense of its impact on the present. It galvanizes young firms to achieve incredible feats powered by purpose and fuelled on belief. It is an asset of the heart perhaps more than the head. It is emotional and requires a simple ingredient to make it work: belief. But it's also a highly volatile and intangible asset. You can't make a provision for it in your forecasts. It can corrode badly and disappear quickly.

The big start-up spirit slayer is the grinding energy required to maintain it. We have always placed the 'always on' mentality at the heart of our business approach. But the concern is for how long and how far this attitude can be taken. How long before a business simply exhausts itself or gets ground down by the day-to-day?

The second assassin is comfort. As you get bigger, people start to buy into the siren belief that somehow size equates to safety. You've done your time, it's somebody else's turn to slog it out on the front line.

It gets worse. As time marches on and teams develop

that weren't there for those start-up days, it becomes harder to focus the organizational mind on maintaining that extreme energy and focus. Irony of ironies, the third enemy at the gates can often be success itself. When we started our firm, a big part of the thinking was that small is smarter, small is more agile, better value and, most importantly, a prize for clients.

Of course, as the market buys this message you grow. It becomes an overriding challenge to avoid becoming exactly that thing you defined yourself against in the early days. How, then, can the campaigner seize the prize of growth without being undermined by its consequences?

The Thermidor Threat

For many campaigners, the essential goal is regime change. They adopt many of the behavioural traits of the revolutionary. They are insurgents, seeking to create new orders in business, impatient with the status quo, seeking an overthrow of stagnant incumbents to create better and more brilliant ways of doing business.

It should come as no surprise, therefore, that the growth pains of the entrepreneur are akin to those identified by some of history's most prominent revolutionaries. The political philosophies of Marx and Engels holds the greatest threat to the revolutionaries to be that of 'Thermidor', adopting the habits and behaviours of the bureaucrats they set out to replace. Their fear, as with the latter period of the French Revolution to which the term refers, was that the pendulum of radicalism ultimately swings to conservatism.

The threat of Thermidor is one that should concern all campaigners. When you start, your purpose and form is at its purest: a streamlined philosophy and methodology for delivering success. You are small, perfectly formed and utterly urgent in everything you do.

A bigger team means people who need to be convinced of the integrity of your purpose as much as the founding team; it means the gradual creep of structures and processes that can be held off no longer as your numbers grow.

'When I think about a business I think about two things,' WANdisco founder David Richards told us. 'Building products and selling them into the market. I don't even want to talk about anything else.

'Then of course when you do an IPO then you need a CFO, you need the office of the CFO and then you need an HR department, none of which is in those two boxes of what you need for a business to execute in the marketplace. But you need those things as well and that's a big challenge, an enormous challenge for any company.'

The importance of Richards' point is that there are many trappings of a growing company that cannot and indeed should not be avoided. What works when your entire team can sit around one desk necessarily cannot once you start to fill an office or more.

Yet as you acquire the accoutrements of a real company, threats abound. What if a bigger team and more bureaucracy means you stop communicating, responding, innovating as you once did? How do you maintain the sense of pace that defines the very best raw start-ups in their launch phase, the urgency to make every hour of every day productive and task-focused?

You must seek to reconcile the best elements of an emerging company, namely agility and responsiveness, with the significant if unwieldy asset of a growing team to service and develop your client base.

Simon Calver, the former CEO of LOVEFiLM and Mothercare, has worked in both corporate and start-up environments, and credits the importance of a lean and agile business environment. 'I passionately believe one area of strategic advantage for smaller companies is speed of decision-making,' he has written.

'At LOVEFiLM I would say one of the most import-ant factors in our cultural success was the office. Everything was completely open plan. We all sat together in the business, running the business. In fact, you could probably throw a single blanket (albeit king-size) and cover the desks of the chief financial officer, chief mar-keting officer, chief technology officer and myself (the chief executive).

'You may think that there is no privacy in this situation, but there were always other meeting rooms people could use if they needed to. And if we needed to make a deci-sion, we would either stand up and chat about it, or pull up a small table and have a quick discussion. Then we could make a decision and move on.'

Whether or not you follow the advice in form or structure, the essence of Calver's point is vitally important. The right visibility and interaction at all levels of your team is essential to ensuring that you avoid developing silos of parallel activity, the enemy of campaigning purpose and in particular innovation.

As you grow, you will inevitably morph from one team that covers all projects into a welter of sub-teams for different elements of the business. This can work perfectly well but only if people are encouraged not to put on the blinkers and to take in and participate in what is going on around them. We have often found that bringing together the entire team for creative sessions or getting people unfamiliar with a project to consult, is the best way of achieving a quick and direct route to goal.

Process: the Enemy of Progress

At heart the campaigner is often the enemy of process, which is what makes the prospect of Thermidor such a terrifying one for them. You won't find many entrepreneurs who embrace or enjoy the prospect of sitting in large-scale meetings for any length of time, but that is exactly what a growing size tends to entail.

Lord Young, the Prime Minister's enterprise adviser, has worked from the heart of government to a series of his own start-ups across a business and political career stretching over five decades.

'If you are an entrepreneur and you're starting out, you

are imaginative, conditions are changing the whole time and you can change your mind three times a day,' he told us.

'Once you get over a certain size you can't do that, then you have to decide a process that takes over because large companies are run by committee. It never gets called a committee but essentially if you decide to do something you're turning around an ocean liner.

'I was executive chairman of Cable and Wireless for five years and we took the profits from £540 million to nearly £1.5 billion. I was bored out of my mind because it was meeting after meeting after meeting.'

Indeed, after retiring from the position aged sixty-five, Lord Young took the only reasonable option for a lifetime entrepreneur, and started again from scratch.

It's an understandable impulse for those who have worked both for themselves and as employees within large companies, where the pursuit of politics over productivity is the antithesis of the can-do mentality of the campaigner. As Lord Young put it to us: 'Every large company I've ever been in or known, the top two or three layers of management spend their time politicking. The business goes on despite them. That's the simple truth, because they're scheming about who's going to get this job or that.'

When you add to internal politics the dead hand of process meetings about meetings – forced moments that obstruct the results they should be expediting – the overall effect is that you lose sight of the important goal: staying on mission, growing the company and achieving profit through purpose.

In the weeds of process, it is the disruptive will and urgency of the campaigner that cuts through and helps deliver results. Some of our best work has come out of meetings that were turned on their head and where best-laid plans were put to one side. You might ruin everyone's Monday morning, but if the net result is to plant a seed that becomes something brilliant, it will have been worth the trouble.

And if you lose the capacity to disrupt, you lose an important weapon in the campaigner's armoury. While your business may never face its ELE (extinction level event), a static brand faces fatal mission creep, death by a thousand cuts until you turn around and wonder how you lost it all.

Fighting the Flab: Staying Lean as You Grow

While growth is the goal of any ambitious and successful business, its side effects can be severe and its impact must be carefully monitored and even countered. We have spent countless weekends working on ideas to ensure the fire continues to burn within our business: coping strategies that ensure the campaign is every bit as vigorous, determined and outlandish as it was the day we opened trading. Here are our top ten:

1. Choice
Decisiveness matters. Building a team that is empowered to make decisions should be at a premium. They may not

get it right all of the time but the process of getting lots of things done leads to momentum.

If you keep too tight a hold on the reins, the chances are you will stifle the life out of the business and your team's will to win. Empowerment and not command-and-control should be your order of the day. It makes for an energetic, committed and unbreakable fighting force, fit to overcome the hurdles that every day throws up.

2. Challenge

Too many people avoid conflict at all costs. Don't be one of them. Where you see things that are not right, move fast to address them, don't shy away from the argument or let the problem fester.

Many seek to circumvent conflict, unwilling to offend, hurt people's feelings, risk making things worse. But that is precisely what you achieve by failing to grasp the problem.

Constructive conflict might sound like a contradiction in terms but it is entirely possible. It means correcting as you go to achieve longer term shifts in behaviour.

Continuous interventions might feel like an exhausting way to run your life; it is, but it is how you keep on track, build culture and ultimately avoid the pitfalls of mission creep.

Downing Street created a team called the Nudge Unit, which aims to achieve organizational change by constant interventions and the restatement of core goals. Every company should have one.

3. Exceptionalism

Always hire people for what they might become, rather than what they have already done. Seek out brilliance in people, and nurture and reward it. What you need is people with a fascination in the world, a thirst for knowledge, a commitment to get better, people who find huge enjoyment and fun in what they do and produce. Every hire should have the potential to be a campaigner. If you accept that not everyone in an organization can be exceptional then the campaigner in you has started to die. Beware the faux-sage advice of those who encourage you to accept that not everyone you hire can be the best.

Accepting that is a damaging concession to a second-rate mentality. Instead, it is our firm ambition that at some point our firm will have become so good that it would never employ us had we sought to join it as employees.

The culture of exceptionalism is not necessarily forgiving, tolerant or based on compromise. But it is based on bringing out the best in people and ensuring a long-term future for the firm.

4. Focus

Give your team daily goals. When we are working on big projects, we instigate a daily meeting we call the 'Five at Five'. A five o'clock meeting about five things you have done that really mattered: to move the campaign forward and to help those around you.

Sitting at their desks, out at meetings and buried in to-do lists, it is all too easy for people to lose sight of the overall mission and indeed the achievements and experience of their fellow travellers. Congregating regularly is an important way of focusing minds on what really matters, as well as championing the success stories and the people who make it happen.

When you get too big to do it with one team, break up the office into corners. Make sure that the celebration of achievement is with you all the way. That way you enshrine a culture where high-performance is the gold standard and acknowledged and rewarded as such. Where you see it, champion it. Where it is failing, move fast to address it.

5. Friendship

As we have said, in our business we hold to the mantra that a family that eats together stays together. As soon as we could, we created a central dining area for our team.

Companies can easily descend into competing self-interests and political machinations, so focus on creating a team that is not only united and high-performing, but where people respect, admire and spend time with each other.

When we hire we think about the personality mix. Could this person be part of a band of brothers and sisters that love the time they spend with each other?

The 2014 LinkedIn Relationships @Work study revealed that 46 per cent of professionals worldwide believe that work friends are important to their overall happiness. LinkedIn found that figure rose massively when applied only to millennials. Friendship, and its importance, is on the rise.

6. Message

Don't dilute it in an attempt to become an 'everyman' brand aiming to be all things to all people. The marketer Seth Godin makes the point, 'tastes like chicken isn't a compliment', for good reason.

We have sought to build the sense of narrative and understanding about the company and its mission at every turn, from films about the firm to adorning the walls of our office with the symbols of campaign victories, awards and photography.

7. Network

The social capital of people matters. There should be no monopoly on contacts. It's not just the job of the boss. It's a part of the fitness to operate of every member of your team. Getting out there and meeting people.

One of the best stationery orders you can make is the reprinting of business cards. It means your team are out and about. Celebrate that.

8. Pack mentality

We arrange our office into pods. Small packs of people who grow, hunt and succeed together. At the heart of the pod is a leader, someone with the authority and skill to champion and grow the people around them.

It builds competition into the wider team, a sense of lean, and the building of elite squads throughout the business.

9. Memory

A slide we like to use in presentations is of two photos of Richard Branson, in the late 1960s and as the familiar face he has become. Remember the journey: the one has remained true to the other.

In our company that means maintaining the start-up ethos, the bootstrap environment where the team feels close to the financial realities of the firm. Comfort and complacency are the enemy; activism and optimism the antidote.

Don't forget where you came from as a company. Similarly, encourage your team to remember why they were hired and never to lose that uniqueness that first caught the eye.

10. Walk

'Let's have a meeting about that meeting.' No! Sit-down meetings are a curse and you can almost always feel the energy leave the room the moment bums hit seats.

When we first started our firm we didn't have an office big enough for a meeting room. Our meetings were called the 'walk in the park'. The perimeter of our local park is exactly a mile. A perfect length for a meeting, and you get some exercise while you are at it.

Takeaways

- Maintaining the campaigning spirit of a start-up is the best way of dealing with the stasis that can afflict larger-sized businesses;

- The growth pains of business are in achieving scale without losing soul – the entrepreneurial urge must be maintained at all costs;
- The big start-up spirit slayer is the grinding energy required to maintain it. The second assassin is comfort, because as you get bigger, people start to buy into the siren belief that somehow size equates to safety;
- How do you maintain the sense of pace that defines the very best raw start-ups in their launch phase, the urgency to make every hour of every day productive and task-focused? We have ten coping strategies: choice, challenge, exceptionalism, focus, friendship, message, network, pack mentality, memory and walk.

Conclusion: The Times They Are A-Changin'

The business stories we have told in *Mission* are those of ideas fulfilled and success realized. But that does not mean their achievements are out of the reach of those yet to pursue their own mission.

Nobody is going to give you permission to quit your job and start a business; or to knock on the door of your chief executive with an idea for how the company you work in could do something better.

Remember this. Many great businesses of our times started from a simple beginning: a good idea that became a clear mission.

Today, that opportunity is readily available: the information, advice and digital tools; the network you never knew was in your grasp; the team of like-minded people ready to be hired or energized from within.

This can prepare you for a world that moves quicker, listens less and demands more. It is a society where the bonds of trust with traditional institutions have dissolved. At the same time the importance of belief has become a vital new currency of business.

You have to work ever harder to stand for something

and to establish the preference in the minds of the people you are selling to.

For some, that level of change is enough to want to pull on the reins, but that horse has well and truly bolted. The world of even a few years ago feels strangely old-fashioned, hierarchical and out of touch with the ambitions of our society in the long aftermath of the financial crash.

We have sought to tell the stories of those people around us who are living a life with a mission. The campaigners who are changing all aspects of the way we live, who are questioning and redefining pillars of the market economy that have stood unchallenged for decades.

And while some might say that this is a story of a rarified few, we would say, in fact, this is a story about us all and the universal opportunity to change things. Technology has levelled the playing field and empowered people in unprecedented numbers to establish their own businesses, control their own fate, to take a grip of their own lives.

Where the graduates of twenty years ago overwhelmingly ended up in big business, today the option of setting up a company or joining a start-up are as available and, in the medium-term, potentially rewarding as following the traditional milk round.

People are relying less and less on traditional institutions to provide jobs, security and prosperity. The opportunity to turn ideas into something meaningful, be that by starting a business or within the company in which you work, has never been greater.

The ability to effect change is not the preserve of a

privileged few, sitting in government or corporate board-rooms. It is an opportunity that is increasingly open to more of us, requiring simply the ambition to change something and the determination to bring a big idea to life. But to do so, you must find your inner campaigner.

The campaigning culture is one that is within your reach: the stories in *Mission* are about everyday people who have done amazing things by sticking to their beliefs, staying true to their mission and learning how to franchise those ideas through campaigning.

Nobody told Joe Gebbia and Brian Chesky of Airbnb that the wheeze they cooked up to make a few hundred dollars to pay their rent could become one of the break-through brands of its generation. When Paul Lindley decided to found what is now the UK's bestselling baby food brand in Ella's Kitchen, by his own admission he knew next to nothing about the food business. It did not take him long to learn, or to identify a new niche into which he has built a global business in under a decade.

At its simplest, what unites true campaigners is that they believe in something. If you have the can-do spirit, that power of belief, then you have the chance to do something amazing. And that doesn't necessarily mean building a company like Google or Whole Foods. What the campaigners we have portrayed in this book exemplify is as much a code for living as a code for business. You can bring the sense of mission they show into almost any human endeavour: be that your next job, an achievement in your personal life, or an academic qualification.

What we have found is that the belief in mission and the activism of campaigning are assets and mentalities at the core of the most exciting, disruptive and influential companies in the world today. Mission grounds you in a fundamental purpose; campaigning gives you a life that can be lived to the full and equips you with momentum, the power to effect change.

Embracing this change and your inner campaigner requires a great deal of bravery, but also another character trait, one that perhaps more than any other defines the people we see as true campaigners: optimism.

In the words of Lord Young, until recently the Prime Minister's enterprise adviser: 'There is one universal characteristic that is possessed by every successful person, and that's positive outlook. It doesn't matter what you do, but is that glass half full or not? If it's half full you see the opportunities and you take them. If it's half empty you never see the opportunities.'

Mission helps fuel this sense of optimism and with it a new class of capitalist, whose defining trait is the ability to get out there: the ability to campaign, to cut through the noise, to win hearts and minds.

It's a set of skills very much in demand. With more information at their disposal than ever before, consumers no longer need to accept what business wants to give them.

The business thinker Peter Drucker made the point many years ago that customers are not prisoners. Never has that observation been truer than it is today. They are more empowered to choose, to effect change, and to stand up for what they want than ever before. And technology has been the great liberator of people, price and performance.

People, because we have a voice that we never had before. From Twitter to TripAdvisor, we can provide our opinion and affect the views of others.

Price, because we can now compare the price of any product anywhere.

And performance, because business lives in a world of intense scrutiny where behaviour is ever easier to scrutinize and to punish.

And if you think this is the end, that where we are today represents the high-water mark of consumer power, think again. This is merely take-off.

The high-growth success stories whose tales we have covered in *Mission* represent the early adopters. Today perhaps the outliers, but very soon their irresistible momentum will become mainstream.

'I guarantee you that ten years from now, there won't be a successful business around that isn't doing some good,' David Jones told us. 'Good is going to happen on every level. Too many chief executives are serious about it, too many young people want to work for companies that do and too many won't abide those who don't.'

The fruits of mission can be seen in many of today's highly successful young companies, but this, and the campaigning mentality that brings it to life, is by no means a mainstream behaviour in business yet.

But to use the oft-said words of Bob Dylan, 'the times they are a-changin'.' Increasingly there is a more distinctive and purposeful voice in the commercial world. It is fuelled by a belief that business can be a force for good in society. That, as John Mackey has said, there is a heroic spirit in business. That mission-based firms can write a new chapter for capitalism.

That is Mission.

Acknowledgements

It all began in San Francisco and the downtown bar at the Battery Club. The Friday night energy of Silicon Valley's entrepreneurial elite. Bold, brave and fearless. A new cast of characters to play out a new chapter in the story of the world of business. *Mission* was manifest.

Writing the book has allowed us to observe up close what it means to be the best in business in a changing world. The friendly enthusiasm with which some of the globe's most exciting entrepreneurs have shared their stories made that task all the more thrilling.

If *Mission* tells the story of what it takes to be the best in business, we have had the privilege of working with the very best to bring that narrative to life.

First and foremost we want to thank our team at Seven Hills who have inspired this project. Our colleague, Josh Davis, has been a tour de force and has worked with us every step of the way. Charlotte Hastings and Jessica de Pree have burned the midnight oil reviewing the drafts that preceded the final copy.

In writing *Mission* we assembled the views and experiences of an inspiring cast of game-changing leaders. For their time and insight we would like to thank Michael Birch, founder of Bebo; John Cridland, director-general of the CBI; Edwina Dunn and Clive Humby, co-founders of dunnhumby; Stephen Fitzpatrick, founder of Ovo Energy; Joe Gebbia, co-founder of Airbnb; Baroness Harding, chief executive of TalkTalk; David Jones, co-founder of One Young World and author of *Who Cares Wins*; Peter Jones CBE, founding *Dragons' Den* panelist; Will King, founder of King of Shaves; Daniel Korski, special adviser to David Cameron; Baroness Lane Fox, founder of last-minute.com and former government digital champion; Sir Terry Leahy, former CEO of Tesco; Paul Lindley, founder of Ella's Kitchen; John Mackey, founder of Whole Foods; Martin McCourt, director at Montagu Private Equity and former CEO of Dyson; Andy McLoughlin, co-founder of Huddle; Frank Meehan, co-founder of SparkLabs Global Ventures; Lord O'Neill, Commercial Secretary to the Treasury and former chief economist at Goldman Sachs; Kathryn Parsons, co-founder of Decoded; Jon Reynolds, co-founder of SwiftKey; David Richards, co-founder and CEO of WANdisco; Kate Robertson, co-founder of One Young World and global president of Havas Worldwide; Lord Rose, chairman of Ocado and former chief executive of Marks & Spencer; Simon Segars, chief executive of ARM Holdings; Russ Shaw, founder of Tech London Advocates; Rohan Silva, founder of Second Home and former No. 10 special adviser; John Vincent, co-founder of Leon Restaurants; Sarah Wood, co-founder of Unruly; and Lord Young of Graffham, enterprise adviser to Prime Minister David Cameron, entrepreneur, and former Secretary of State for Trade and Industry.

ACKNOWLEDGEMENTS

To Lord Young, we would like to offer a special salute. His wisdom, vigour and friendship have been an inspiration.

We have also been greatly privileged to support His Royal Highness the Duke of York's work in championing British enterprise, and would like to offer our thanks to him and his team, notably Amanda Thirsk, his private secretary.

The Seven Hills advisory board members warrant mention for their support and encouragement: the broadcaster Katie Derham and enterprise champions Lord Bilimoria of Chelsea, Ed Wray, Oli Barrett and Paul Firth.

Along the way we have had the advice of some great people including Tom Bromley, Emma de Vita and Rachel Bridge. And we would like to thank Joel Rickett, Richard Lennon, Zoe Bohm and the team at Portfolio Penguin for their brilliant insight, patience and enthusiasm.

Finally, to our wives and children. Our mission is you.

MICHAEL HAYMAN & NICK GILES
July 2015